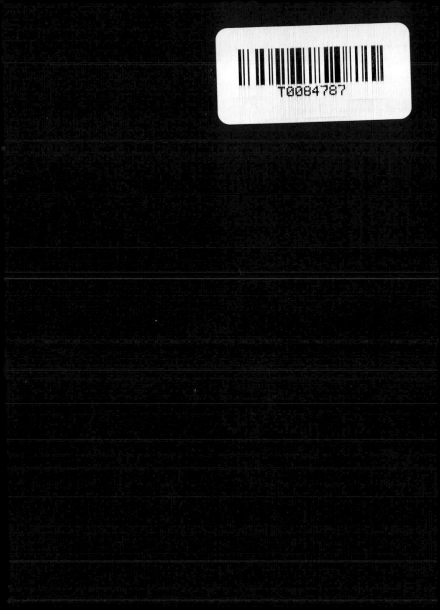

Jewish Journeys

For my parents
Michael Leigh *z'l* and Sonia Leigh.
With love, respect and gratitude.

Jewish Journeys

by
Jeremy Leigh

 ArmchairTraveller

HAUS PUBLISHING
London

Copyright © 2006 Jeremy Leigh

First published in Great Britain in 2006 by Haus Publishing
Limited, 26 Cadogan Court, Draycott Avenue, London SW3 3BX

The moral rights of the author have been asserted.

A CIP catalogue record for this book is available from the
British Library

ISBN 1-904950-39-6

Typeset in Garamond 3 by MacGuru Ltd
Printed and bound by Graphicom in Vicenza, Italy
Jacket illustrations courtesy of Getty Images

Contents

Jewish Journeys

Self:
Personal Reflections on Jewish Journeys

What does one pack for a Jewish journey? I have always been puzzled by the things people pack in their suitcases, especially if the journey is one that may connect them to their Jewishness. A common stereotype is that the reason why Jews played violins is because pianos were too cumbersome to carry on their endless journeys. When they left Egypt, escaping slavery, there was no time to pack so they took unleavened bread. But what of the deliberate Jewish journeys, more recognizable to myself as a tour guide? Definitely a warm hat for Vilna after October and sunglasses for Cordoba from March onwards. Certainly religious head coverings for cemeteries and synagogues if one is that way inclined. Packing the address book of the local Jewish community would depend on being committed to the present as well as the past. Maps are complicated since the layout of previous Jewish space has been swamped and built over too many times to find contemporary maps that useful. Someone once suggested shaving foam is good for deciphering old gravestones – smear all over, then wipe off the top level leaving the shaving foam in the thin indentations of letters. So much depends on what one expects to happen on such a journey. The Israeli poet Yehuda Amichai offers a different suggestion.

> *Jewish Travel. As it is written, "I will lift up*
> *mine eyes unto the hills,*
> *from whence cometh my help": not a hike to see a*
> *tall mountain in*
> *all its glory,*
> *nor to climb to rejoice in the vistas of Nature,*
> *but a hike with a purpose, to seek help from the*
> *high heavens …*
> *Not hikers singing, knapsacks on their*
> *shoulders, but rather*

a congregation praying with "clean hands and a
pure heart,"
not strong bodies and sturdy legs ...[1]

A Jewish journey may not require any equipment at all, only a state of mind, purpose or a pure heart.

For the last twenty years I have worked in various capacities around the issue of Jewish journeys. As a Jewish history teacher and travel guide I have accompanied many groups to locations and sites that make up the Jewish story. In preparation for these group experiences, I have also spent significant periods of time alone, trudging around those same locations trying to tease out a story in my mind that will draw students and participants to a richer engagement with the Jewish drama. Yet throughout, there is one plain and simple truth that shines through time and time again and that is that journeys are about more than travel. They comprise the thrilling, challenging, at times dangerous and at other times depressing, encounter with the world beyond. Most importantly however, they unlock an encounter with oneself.

Travel literature is a literature of dialogue, presenting a conversation between the traveller and the place. Implicit is a tension or even a struggle to decide who has the primary role, the place itself with all the dramas that unfold there, or the narrator, the traveller whose experience of the place is mediated. One could argue this as a moral argument to decide whose rights are greater, those of the place to be presented honestly and without bias in its own terms and with as little editorial as possible, or those of the visitor who can only see what they see and feel what they feel.

The selections of literature presented in this book are a personal collection of 'voices' from places and times in the Jewish past from which I find it hard to escape. The sad reflection of Nahmanides writing from Jerusalem to his son in Girona cannot but whisper in my ear when I've walked, over 700 years later, through the enchanting streets of Girona's Old Town. And absolutely nothing about modern-day Vilna makes any sense without the haunting and passionate description of the town by Chaim Grade as he returns after the war. It is as if one is intruding, listening to the private cries of grief of a mourner uttered over the grave of someone who was deeply loved. For me this is the essence of the dialogue that travel offers, the possibility to go beyond, look behind and underneath to find points of connection that turn the experience of travel into a true journey.

People and Places

The physical locations of Jewish journeys demand a degree of imagination beyond the hills and vistas of Nature. They include the sites of cafés where great Yiddish writers once sat and the remains of fountains and streams where Spanish Jews and Muslims met to recite poetry and discuss philosophy. They encapsulate the life and times of a whole people, their dramas, inspirations, sufferings and celebrations. Journeying to the locations where these people lived is a trigger to engage with their worlds and an opportunity to comprehend the meaning of the interaction between people and place. This is true whether it is between continent and continent, home and exile, slavery and freedom, East and West, or simply between community and community – the journey and the reflection on the journey are attempts to engage.

Fifteen years ago a friend found himself running out of petrol when driving to the north of England to attend a Jewish youth camp, late on a Friday afternoon. Fortunately, a signpost soon appeared pointing to a petrol station off the motorway by the city of York. An observant and religious Jew, he was concerned that the journey be finished before sundown or else he would be breaking the laws of the Jewish Sabbath that forbid motorized travel on the day of rest. Unfortunately, as the indicator light flashed, he was hit by the force of Jewish memory with the recollection that 800 years earlier, almost the entire Jewish community of York had committed suicide in the royal castle to avoid death at the hands of a mob who demanded they convert or be killed. Legend has it that, since then, the Jewish authorities placed the city of York under *herem*, a ban of excommunication, forbidding any Jew from setting foot in that accursed place. But none of this could change the simple reality that the fuel light was flashing, the clock was ticking its way towards sundown and the only chance of help was to be found in the domain of the excommunicated city. In the pre-mobile phone period of the twentieth century, he had no choice but to drive around the ring road in desperate search for a telephone box to call the rabbinic authority in London. However, down in London the matter could not be resolved that quickly since the person in charge was an Israeli educator who had been seconded to the organization for two years. He was fully up to speed on matters of religious Zionist ideology but somewhat deficient in matters relating to the legacy of twelfth-century Jews in Yorkshire. Unable to resolve the question himself he called his rabbinic supervisor in Israel for advice. I have no idea how many levels it reached nor how many laps of the ring road there were until the decision came through, but eventually the matter was decided. The petrol should be purchased in York, with or without the ban, the Sabbath should not be desecrated and the journey could continue ...

Fifteen years later I remain intrigued by the episode since it highlights the complex challenge of defining Jewish journeys. A mundane car journey was transformed into an engagement with the totality of Jewish experience. At stake were pressing questions of religious observance against the powerful backdrop of Jewish memory. I recognize an ambiguity as to which element actually created the 'Jewishness' of the journey: the individual Jew, in the form of my friend whose particular worldview demanded such behaviour; 'the group' in the form of the Jewish People and their experiences, their rabbinic leaders and institutions that interpreted the legacy of York; 'history' that bequeathed another chapter of martyrdom to later generations; maybe even God in whose name the Jews had, at least on the surface of things, been killed and in defence of whose honour the Jews chose to die rather than convert.

On the one hand all of this adds up to a complicated interpretation of what was meant to have been a straightforward drive up the M1. On the other, it highlights the remarkable potential of travel, to expose new insights and to shine a light on things that may have been present before but could not be seen. One thing is certain, it uncovers the complexity of connecting Jews with places.

Consciously or unconsciously, everyone has a place, somewhere that locates them in time and space. For some people that place does not actually exist yet. Imagining it or being aware of its potential existence provides a point of reference for their being. The poet Yankev Yitzchok Segal (mentioned later in the last chapter) lived almost his entire life in Montreal writing poetry that was in so many ways about his true place, in the town of his childhood. On an altogether different level I remember the moving experience of seeing a participant in a group I was guiding in Poland literally discover a place that she had been distant from for so many years; she had grown up in a Jewish suburb of London and not in Poland, a place that she had not returned to for over 50 years. The encounter with the sites of a Yiddish-speaking world long gone and with the symbols of the tourist reality in twenty-first-century Poland, brought back years of alienation and distance to a point of connection and belonging. Another man in the same group, similarly far from his Jewish roots, found himself singing whole songs in Yiddish learned in childhood. These are the journeys of meaning, the ones that connect places with the inner sense of self.

In my own case, I must confess that things were a little more complicated in the other direction, suffering no dislocation that could produce poetic reflections of another place or long years of alienation to reconnect with. In fact, I grew up with a profound sense of a 'non place' and all the disappointments that it represented. Born and raised in North-West London, there came a point in my teenage years when I realized I was living in distinctly unremarkable times. My grandfather, like the grandfathers of most of my Jewish friends, emigrated from Eastern Europe to Britain at the beginning of the twentieth century. My father was evacuated during the war, did National Service, was the first person in his family to go to university and became a rabbi in a fast-growing Jewish community. In itself this was no more or less remarkable than many other first-generation children of Jewish immigrants but it was sufficient to create a recognition that something had gone before me. These were historical markers, 'events' and places, recognizable moments that could be read about in books.

My maternal grandfather died young but not before introducing his children to *Hashomer Hatzair,* a Marxist wing of the Zionist movement. From the little I know of him, I doubt he was the political revolutionary type, but in the spirit of many people associated with such movements, he seemed more the 'verbal revolutionary', talking a lot about the idea but not necessarily doing it. By the time he died, however, my two uncles were living on *kibbutzim* (co-operative communities) in Israel, both married to survivors of the Holocaust from continental Europe. Since we never travelled abroad, it meant I grew up knowing about, imagining and yet never seeing a part of the family who lived in the mythological country called Israel, with an uncle who fought in the wars and who farmed the land. It was all enough to generate a notion of time and place in my adolescent mind. But critically they were times and places that were far more interesting than my own, realizing as I did that Stanmore was imbued with no romantic associations with the past and certainly no revolutionary potential. Reading or simply hearing of recent Jewish history, positive, tragic or just challenging, simply reinforced a sense of disappointment. Stanmore of the 1980s was never going to be Vilna of 1905, *fin-de-siècle* Vienna or 1920s Tel Aviv. Lacking swamps to drain, I internalized early on that history happened elsewhere.

Like many of my contemporaries, the one route into the drama of history came via the Zionist youth movements that had been established two generations earlier to re-assert the Jewish national spirit within the consciousness of Jewish immigrant youth. These were socio-educational campaigns to resist the conformism and anglicizing tendencies of the Anglo-Jewish establishment. Through summer camps, weekly meetings and, from the 1960s onwards, through visits to Israel, these youth movements galvanized thousands of young Anglo-Jews into seeing themselves as part of the Jewish nation. It was a type of fantasy which allowed teenagers to imagine they really were pioneers of the new generation.

For my part, the fantasy dovetailed nicely with my 'no-Jewish-revolution-in-Stanmore' teenage *angst*. The youth movement finally enabled me to travel, first to Israel and then to Eastern Europe. From that point there could be no going back. Of course it could have been late teenage identity-formation overload, but frankly who cares. All I know is I succeeded in making a connection between the past and the present that was happening around me.

There was an incredible moment roughly two minutes after leaving the airport terminal the first time I visited Poland, as part of a delegation of Jewish youth movement leaders. The road signs looked remarkably like the chapters in my Jewish history books from university. Apparently, people still lived in Warsaw, as they did in Kielce, Krakow and Lodz. Furthermore it was possible to go to these places. Travelling down the respective motorways to these places I was on a great historical fairground ride. Inevitably the trip also generated the reverse mental process. On arriving in Warsaw it was endlessly frustrating to acknowledge that the Ghetto Uprising was over and I could play no role in it. Mordechai Anilewicz (the commander of the Ghetto revolt) had become a street name. To make it worse, people actually lived their everyday lives around the 'holy' sites where the uprising took place, somehow deflating its sense of grandeur.

The same thing happened in 1988 when I visited the Soviet Union, like the many other youth movement activists anxious to offer solidarity with Jews denied the right to emigrate to Israel. I was asked to deliver a lecture to Jews in Vilna, the capital of Soviet-controlled Lithuania and the city my family had originated from. The inside of the lecture hall was not that dissimilar to the lecture halls in London where I was studying. Furthermore, given the fact that the Nazis and the Soviets between them had managed to erase all but the smallest remnant of pre-war Jewish building, there seemed very little to look at. Yet the context of the environment, namely being on a journey to another Jewish world – one that just two generations earlier had been the home of my

16

family – which was at that very moment fighting for its rights, was an inspiration.

Putting aside the frustrations of the humdrum nature of late twentieth-century North-West London Jewish suburbia, I recognize that these were pivotal moments in which the basic contours of Jewish travel were established in my mind. Journeying to places where the Jewish drama had once unfolded meant to acknowledge, right from the start, that imagination and feeling are critical. In actual fact, Jewish journeys are very often about the invisibility of the story, the reality of looking very closely at something that is not there. For the last twenty years, either as a volunteer youth leader or later as a history teacher, I have grappled with the challenge of taking groups on Jewish journeys to sites where something significant once happened. How does one generate excitement and historical identification with the story of the place with so little to see or so much going on around elsewhere? It is a fine thing to bring enthusiastic Jewish travellers to Cordoba in Andalusian Spain to retell of the great period of Muslim–Jewish dialogue in the tenth century, but how is that possible when there are only two sites and a street sign to look at, compounded by the tense state of Jewish–Muslim relations at the present moment in history? Jewish Mainz or Jewish Worms remain walking tours I have devised and that no group has ever requested since it would seem that the Jewish travelling public cannot relate to the distinct episodes of medieval Ashkenazi Jewish history that these sites represent. Or else they recognize there is only so much one can squeeze out of a medieval Jewish cemetery, surrounded by modern apartment buildings, shops and a motorway on both sides.

There are two exceptions to this frustration. The first is when I am alone, pounding the streets of Jewish Europe doing research. In those long hours learning the routes of walking tours that I hope will one day be shared with others, I can indulge any fantasy I want, forging tight points of connection between past and present. Thankfully I no longer try to imagine actually being there. In its place is the belief in the intrinsic value of establishing or re-establishing connections with actual places where the meta-journey of Jewish history once passed by.

The other moment when the frustration subsides is in relation to home. Since the early 1990s, home has been Jerusalem where, with the best will in the world, one cannot complain there is not enough to look at or that history has finished. In fact, for the overly zealous Jewish history enthusiast, there is no chance of disconnecting. Put another way, it means my personal Jewish journey is ever-present, even in the context of everyday life.

Jewish 'Munro Bagging': Collecting Jewish Journeys

There is a convention amongst the British mountaineering community known as 'Munro Bagging', which describes the pursuit of climbing all the Scottish mountains above 3,000 feet, known as 'Munros'. It is an intriguing challenge combining the recognized, if at times eccentric, desire to collect things with a recognition that mountains are very special and challenging types of places. To have taken them on suggests a prowess at conquering both the physical and spiritual power of nature.

I have never climbed a single Munro, although I would dearly love to do so. What I have done, though, is run around some of the most remarkable sites of Jewish history in Europe. In all places, home or away, I have to start the day with exercise. As an aspiring marathon runner (although highly unlikely to ever become one), my days habitually begin by huffing and puffing my way through the streets or on a treadmill for just over an hour each morning. There was a time when I reserved that early morning slot for the religious requirements of prayer, but since theological crises have chipped away at that resolve, my soul lies neglected and the time is used instead to attend to the needs of the body. Given the deep and bitter struggle between Jewish and Hellenistic culture, I have no doubt my ancestors would condemn me as a traitor. At any rate, in the last number of years I have 'bagged' Jewish historical locations across the continent of Europe, traversing over 2,000 years of history on the way. The three passions for history, journeys and physical exercise can all be rolled into one neat package.

Suitably attired and mentally revved, I have pushed myself around the sites of Rome. I have observed the points along the River Tiber where Jewish diplomats arrived from Jerusalem in the second century before Jesus to forge relations with the emerging power that would eventually engulf them. Was this the same spot, I wonder, where chained and exiled Jewish captives disembarked following their defeat by Rome 200 years later? I have also jogged, paced and sprinted the streets of medieval Mainz and Worms where the monumental communities of the Rhine established the Rabbinic academies that would define so much of Ashkenazi Jewish culture. Marvelling along the way at their intellectual prowess, it is hard to shut out the thought that it was possibly along these very same streets that eleventh-century Crusaders massacred those same Jews who refused to accept the Cross. In a similar vein, I once got lost passing the former Hebrew engraved tombstones that were used to build the walls around Barcelona's magnificent cathedral.

The Jews were expelled from there in the fifteenth century but the Hebrew stones remain to bear witness to the excesses of the Church at that time.

Unfortunately, the minute size of the Venice Ghetto offers little chance for increasing one's pulse rate since the Venetian authorities only granted one small island to enclose the Jewish community in the sixteenth century. One has far more chance of getting fit going round the old and larger cities of Cordoba, Vilna or Wroclaw, all of which possess rich histories to keep the mind occupied. To get round the Jewish sites of Berlin is to acknowledge the symbolic as well as the physical distance that Jews travelled to get beyond the confines of the traditional community in the Scheunenviertel and out into the wide expanses of the city in Charlottenburg. Bagging Jewish Berlin requires only 400 years of historical memory but almost a marathon's-worth of physical distance.

I would like to stress that the significance of this type of Jewish 'Munro Bagging' lies not in the thrill of simple 'collecting' ('almost done the Rhineland but haven't even started on the Galician *Shtetls*'), but more about the questions it throws up. Sites of the significant past presume a certain degree of respect, even awe. How then does any contemporary visitor, attired in either running shorts and trainers or holiday gear, appropriately approach such places when that past is long over? Instinctively, we contemporary Jewish travellers hope to find something to look at or at least a significant place to feel connected. It is probably the much talked-about 'search for authenticity' that, according to many commentators, defines the contemporary Western man/woman.

Walking the modern streets of Worms, Cordoba or Rome is to a degree mundane and ordinary. Traffic, municipal street cleaners and tacky shops all reinforce that ordinary feel and remind me that these places carry no organic sacredness or power. They are only significant because we choose to make them so by remembering what once happened there. Therefore I can enjoy collecting jogging routes around the great sites of Jewish Europe as a way of acknowledging their ordinariness as sites, focusing at one and the same time on 'history' as well as on breathing technique and muscle strain. Focusing on history and meaning is not to forget what existed there as well as acknowledging my own status as a Jew living in a radically different period of time. Personally I cannot help feeling mildly smug at the outcome of history which enables me to return freely to all these places with my Israeli passport, and whilst there gloat inwardly at the miracle of Jewish survival.

This type of interaction between past and present inspired by travel is replicated in potentially different ways at home.

Jerusalem I

The greatest mistake in thinking about journeys is the belief that they require moving long distances to the domain of someone else's story and not seeking the dramas of one's own home environment. In actual fact it is more than a mistake and is more like a tragedy since it reflects a devaluing of the essence of one's own reality. Leading participants on walking tours of their own city, telling stories of their own family's history, has on occasions appeared faintly surreal to me. The overriding impression when observing such groups is a combination of complete ignorance and high levels of fascination. For instance, in the case of London, I am always puzzled why, for so many Jews, the straightforward journey down the Jubilee Line to the East End is the effective equivalent of crossing the Pyrenees. Admittedly these are easy words for a Jewish history teacher, but it still requires effort to find the sites and create the story.

Personally, nothing compares with the challenge of running in Jerusalem, which has been my home for the last thirteen years. The term 'home' would probably suggest that it is not part of the journey, not a travel experience since one normally travels from and to home, so precluding it from the journey itself. I would assert that travel is all about home for precisely that very reason. The focal point of all journeys is home, since that is what defines a person and invariably the focus of their life. Sunbathers on a beach in Spain are knowingly or unknowingly relating to their need to get away from home, as are those on religious pilgrimages who wish to differentiate between the sacred and the ordinary. In my own case, leaving Britain for Israel almost 100 years after my grandfather first arrived in the East End from Russia, means that going to Israel can only be regarded as another stage on a journey. It may be called home with all that this normally implies – the newspaper is delivered daily, we have a washing machine and everything I possess is located here – but it is still a part of the journey. In fact, given the short space of time that has elapsed since the United Nations established Israel as a Jewish 'home'-land and the fact that the vast majority of the Jewish population have been here for no more than three generations and many for less, we are all living out of suitcases of a sort. Indeed, on that level, few people can really call it home. On another level of course, this is precisely where the Jewish People was born, where its national memory is bound up and national identity is focused. We are on the journey of reconnecting the mythical notion of home with a physical one. In the meantime there also many points of absurdity. Take for example, running.

Running in Jerusalem presents its own challenges, not least the fact the city is built on hills. However, there is also an overabundance of history which can be difficult for orienting oneself, securing oneself or ensuring one does not offend others. One must be on guard all the time for fear of getting too close to the past or to the present, the religious holy or the secular sacred. Nobody runs around the Western Wall, along the Via Dolorosa or up and down the Temple Mount/ Haram al-Sharif, but that is not the point. These are officially sacred spots as opposed to unofficial ones. Quite apart from the ever-present national rivalries between Jew and Arab, the everyday life of the city is constantly at odds with the ever-appearing symbols of memory and meaning. For instance, if one runs too far in one direction, one must confront the site of the Separation Fence which simultaneously promises protection against death at the hands of suicide bombers at the same time as fundamentally disrupting the daily lives of local Palestinians.

On another level there is the challenging question of finding the appropriate etiquette for running in areas where large signs are hung by the local Ultra Orthodox residents imploring inappropriately (immodestly) attired visitors not to enter. Too much exposed flesh does not sit well with these covered-up Jews and so is out of bounds for Jerusalem runners for the eight months of the year when tracksuits would melt in the overpowering sun. To find a running route is to tease out the fault lines between the seams of an overburdening history. One can run along the uninspiringly-named Highway Number One, between the outer edges of Ultra Orthodox Jewish Mea Shearim and the fringes of Arab East Jerusalem. This road, which was once the cease-fire line between 1948 and 1967, remains a kind of no man's land of symbols.

Then there is my own somewhat odd neighbourhood. As an economic 'refugee' from the nicer parts of town, my home is situated in Armon Hanatziv, a shoddily-constructed suburb on the south side of the city. Built by the Likud government in the 1980s, every street is named after dubious 'heroes' of the pre-state right-wing Jewish underground, reflecting the desire of contemporary planners to ensure we suburban folk live 'our' history on a daily basis. I live just off 'Ascent to the Gallows' street. Despite the claims of my postal address, I have never been convinced that my ancestors dreamt for 2,000 years of returning to this small patch of land. When Yehuda Halevi, arguably the greatest of the medieval Spanish Hebrew poets wrote 'My heart is in the East but I am in the uttermost West', I doubt he was dreaming of Armon Hanatziv.

Armon Hanatziv backs onto Jebel Mukaber and Sur Bakher, two Arab villages incorporated into the city after the 1967 war. Almost all the local taxi drivers in the area come from these villages which means that as a short-sighted non-driver, there are many journeys I take into the city centre in my neighbours' cabs. Given that there are few points of contact between Jews and Arabs in the city, I regard myself lucky to have developed friendships across the national ethnic divide. Beyond everyday chat, the depth of relationship extends to good wishes at holiday times, mutual concerns for children and condolences for family bereavements. We have not got as far as eating in each other's homes yet but since no-one is planning on leaving the area, anything is possible. In terms of discussion, luckily we have already discussed the issue of the status of the land on which the neighbourhood is built, namely part village grazing land, part unclaimed and unused scrub. This only leaves everyday politics to get in the way of the budding friendship, especially given that there is no everyday politics here that is not built on a century of conflict. 'Strange', 'absurd', 'hopeful' and 'depressing' are all suitable words for describing the conversation between us over the last number of years, as all of us have watched the same explosions at night, heard the same helicopters flying overhead and narrowly missed being killed by the same suicide bombers. Yet, there still remains so much that is unsaid. In theory, our journeys are just journeys, from the neighbourhood to school or to the gym. On the other hand they are tortuous routes between subjects and away from subjects, cushioned by the unstated but obvious desire to retain friendships until at least the next journey.

Strangely the one topic of conversation never broached, but not for any political reason, is the incredible view as we leave the neighbourhood. The road glides past the *tayelet* (promenade) built along the ridge that was once populated by goats and their shepherds and is now paved over to benefit tourists. There, just 200 metres from home lies *the* picture postcard view of Jerusalem, with the dazzling golden dome standing out as the most obvious marker. Here one sees how the West turns to the East (or vice versa), how the city rises out of the desert and where three monotheistic civilizations have their most sacred sites. This overlooks the spot where Abraham did not sacrifice his son Isaac. It was probably the mountain over which pilgrims came in days of old bringing their first fruits to the Temple below. It is for this view that Jews have yearned for 2,000 years. This is one of the most hotly-contested cities in the world, and yet from above looking down it all looks so peaceful. To be perfectly honest we probably do not talk about it because what could one possibly say – 'Nice view?'

The point is that living in Jerusalem is a constant battle to retain a sense of normality in the quicksand of historical symbols that lie in wait everywhere.

Jerusalem II: Seven Naked Men in a Jerusalem Shower

In the last few years my Jerusalem Jewish journeys have been filtered through a daily encounter with six naked men in the shower of my Jerusalem gym. History and holiness outside notwithstanding, it is a hilly city making it a disaster for runners with low levels of motivation. Yet that does not stop the characters who make up the story of this strange city congregating in such semi-public spaces bringing their stories with them. In my case this means a small cast, who, in my mind at least, represent a distinct type of journey. The luxury of being in a gym after eight in the morning in a society where most people are already at work or school means that one encounters only retirees or those in professions that permit such a lifestyle. Freelance tour guides/teachers fall into this category and explains why I am the youngest runner showering at this time of the morning.

West Jerusalem's YMCA is a grand and sprawling affair built in Oriental style, opposite the famous King David Hotel which conversely was built in markedly Central European style at the same time in the early twentieth century. For the travel/culture obsessive such as myself, I cannot help enjoying the idea of turning 'eastward' into the building where the gym is situated alongside a guest house and an Arab-Jewish kindergarten, thereby leaving the opulent 'West' (i.e. the King David) for the visiting wealthy and diplomatic corps for whom the King David is the natural home. And there, in this Arab-owned and run institution, I meet the same six characters in the shower.

Firstly there are four men aged seventy-plus who were born in Morocco, Tunisia and Iraq and who arrived in Israel at various points in the first fifteen years of Israel's short history. These men talk about two things and two things only: football and politics. In Israel these pursuits are actually linked since the main soccer clubs are naturally affiliated with political institutions. The politics are distinctly right-wing. The four years in which we have met each morning has coincided with the wave of violence in the region that has left thousands dead on both sides and deep despair in the hearts of all. The four live near the market which has taken a larger than average share of the blasts. Following one such display of carnage, they still managed to argue about an unfairly-awarded penalty. However, the one thing that they all agree on is that there is no-one to trust in the world except ourselves. 'Ourselves' is a euphemism for Jews, or rather Israeli Jews, but to be precise *Mizrachi* (lit. 'Oriental') Israeli Jews who hail from Middle Eastern and North African countries, since it was always Ashkenazi (European) Jews who dominated the élites of Israel and by extension excluded the *Mizrachi* newcomers. They are the very embodiment of people for whom 'place' is central to their lives. They never miss an opportunity to remind all who care to listen where they originate from and why they are implicitly more chosen than the average member of the 'Chosen People'.

On Mondays, Thursdays (the days for reading the Torah in synagogue) and Friday, the day before the Sabbath, there is much humming of the tunes from their respective synagogues, turning the shower into a repository of musical traditions from across the Jewish world. Down the corridor and away from the shower, a large Ashkenazi gentleman who wears a skullcap even when he exercises, hums the same prayers but according to a different *nusach* (musical tradition). The corridor separates the traditions of sacred music and symbolically several thousand miles of Jewish historical space.

Intermingled in this crowd is a small quiet man with a blue number tattooed on his arm, informing all that he was in Auschwitz-Birkenau. In fact he hails from a *shtetl* near the Polish industrial city of Lodz. (It took me two years to decide whether I could ask him where he came from and I am still unsure whether he really wanted to tell me.) The tattoo is an unspoken symbol but one that my overly historical mind cannot ignore. How does he feel having to reveal his tragic story every time he comes to the gym? Does he ever forget it as one does a regular body mark? Has his attitude to the tattoo changed over time? Does he look out for others with similar tattoos? To what degree does he relate the tattoo with a time and place in history? He was not fortunate enough to be born in a part of the Jewish world where the Nazis did not reach, such as the men in the other cubicles. And most importantly, is he any more aware than I am that the sixth man in the shower is the Jerusalem correspondent of one of Germany's leading newspapers? I should stress that the journalist has lived successfully in Jerusalem for the last ten years, suffering its ups and downs with us all. I am sure he is acutely aware of the complexities of having such an identity in this intense city and equally aware that as much as one can separate the person from the symbol, there are times when things are just too complicated. This may be one such moment.

The shower is every bit a part of the journey, albeit a symbolic one. The players originate in all parts of the modern and ancient Jewish drama. Consciously or unconsciously they bring culture, politics and history to the daily workout. To understand them, one must know that the Jewish community of Iraq is 2,500 years old and its significance in terms of the creation of Jewish culture outstrips almost everywhere apart from the Land of Israel. One must also travel to Spain to learn of the rich cultural heritage it bequeathed to its post-1492 (the year of Expulsion) diaspora who eventually joined the existing communities in North Africa and, in the case of my men in the shower, in Morocco and Tunisia. This extends to acknowledging the circumstances of these same Jews who, after living in Arab countries for hundreds of years, found life untenable after the creation of the Jewish State. One must know that Jews have been living in Poland since the thirteenth century although in the case of my shower partner, in Lodz from the nineteenth century. My roots lie in Lithuania which is to the north of Poland and carries nuanced differences of cultural and religious expression filtered through the two generations of Anglicization. And of course there is the ever-present question of the relations between Jews and non-Jews which has varied according to conditions of time. For my right-wing shower partners who all speak Arabic, the Arab society of their youth gives them, or so they believe, perfect credentials to manage the Middle East Peace Process. I wonder what my friend from Germany would have to say about that.

I am sharply aware of them when I travel to Jewish sites around the world. Making a journey, leaving home for another destination, sharpens the mind on what one is leaving. Jogging my way around the grey streets of Lodz on a cold morning could only ever evoke the sense of my man in the gym. Similarly trips to Germany, although to date I have never been to Morocco, Tunisia or Iraq. Standing before a group by the port in Barcelona, with the beautiful blue sea behind me, talking about the impact of the expulsion of Jews from Spain, always leads to the subject of where the exiles went. Playing my group a piece of Sephardi music to illustrate the idea of cultural legacy, the carrying of identity and memory from one location to another, suddenly brings the Moroccan and Tunisian story into focus.

The poetics of such associations all became so strangely dislocated in one bizarre incident, which sounds too ridiculous and coincidental to be true. It is, I vouch, all true. Having never won a raffle or a lottery I do not ordinarily believe in coincidence since my lottery numbers never coincidentally come up. But in this absurd story they did.

There I was guiding a group of students around the site of the Wannsee Conference where Reinhard Heydrich and other leading Nazi bureaucrats gathered in January 1942 to finalize the details of the Final Solution. Waiting patiently to go into the actual room where the meeting took place, I heard Hebrew and suddenly the Jewish journey became more absurd than ever.

'*Ani lo ma'amin, ma ata ose po?*' ('I don't believe it, what on earth are you doing here?').

I was tempted to remark that they looked so different with their clothes on but held back, making do with similar expressions of dismay and Israeli-style slapping of backs and palms, which I really cannot do convincingly. The gym ensemble of Moroccan,

Tunisian and Iraqi Jewish sacred music hummers had come sightseeing to Berlin!

After they had left and words such as 'mad', 'incredible' and 'coincidence' had left me, I could not get over the fact that they would go there in the first place. Jews should of course visit such places, but in truth few go to Germany, fewer still to Berlin and those that do are usually on organized educational trips or are survivors from the city returning after many years of absence. What was it that possessed them to be there and why did it happen that we should extend our daily Jewish journey into one in that macabre room in Berlin? On deeper reflection, as well as being the sort of coincidence I would normally believe to be impossible, it struck me just what a remarkable moment had occurred there. Two clusters of Jews originally hailing from such different parts of the Jewish world and yet currently living in the historic capital of the Jewish People, meet up in a site of the Jewish story, thousands of miles from home. I would like to think that similar situations will one day occur for Ashkenazi Jews in locations off the beaten track in Casablanca and Baghdad.

The intense microcosm of the gym shower in Jerusalem is in itself a powerful image, representing the ambiguous nature of place in the Jewish journey. One room, seven men and at least three continents of experience. But what about the Jewish journeys that are not confined to small spaces, where a whole expanse exists to create the Jewish journey?

Into the Wilderness I: Journey to Saskatchewan

A taxi driver collected me from the airport in Saskatchewan's capital city, Regina, in the heart of the Canadian prairies. Having already flown for two hours and still in central Canada, I had another four hours' drive due south to reach my destination. Taking some time out from Europe, I was to write a travel book telling the story of Jewish Canada in chosen locations across that vast country. The familiar immigrant stories of Montreal and Halifax had now given way to the journey out west.

Allowing for tiredness and the loss of poetic inspiration, the journey nevertheless remains in my mind as the single dullest of my life, passing neither tree nor hill, just endless miles of what appeared to be the same never-ending field. Like the pilot who switches on the 'fasten your seatbelt' sign half-an-hour before actually landing, the driver told me we would 'soon' be in Hirsch, at least 40 minutes before we were. Then suddenly, appearing literally out of nowhere was a 'field' (a fenced-off area in the larger field that is southern Saskatchewan) with a sign announcing to all who drove by that this was Hirsch and here was its cemetery. A large *Magen David* (Star of David) stood aloft advertising to the wind that this was a Jewish cemetery.

In 1892, the wealthy German Jewish philanthropist Baron de Hirsch donated $35,000 to establish a farming colony in western Canada, increasing by one the list of new destinations for Jews pouring out of the Russian Empire. Far from New York's Lower East Side or London's East End, a cluster of aspiring Jewish farmers came to Saskatchewan. Having largely speaking been scholars and merchants for the last 2,000 years, this was a brave undertaking for Jews with little or no farming experience but soon the Canadian prairies had a few hundred Yiddish speakers trying to grow wheat. The rest of the story is, as they say 'retold in the annals of Israel'. Suffice to say the reason for my journey was to find the only two Jews remaining from that time.

Having never married, the Kleinman brothers remained in Hirsch for their entire lives: caring for the cemetery; burying the occasional former resident who wished this remarkable location to be their final resting place and simply attesting to the fact that Hirsch was once a Jewish farming colony. Now in their eighties they were charming men, for whom nothing was too much and for whom kindness and politeness seemed to be their defining characteristics. As we sat in their kitchen recalling former times, the conversation turned to me and my home in Israel. And then one of them said it:

'You know, when one of those suicide bombs go off in Israel, we feel it right here, as if we were there'.

'Really', I mumbled.

There in Hirsch, Saskatchewan, the ultimate Canadian 'place beyond', distance was no barrier to Jewish solidarity. For a moment, all notions of Jewish space were unified and home seemed very close indeed. As a moment on a personal Jewish journey I am constantly challenged by that comment since it seems simultaneously inspiring and also ridiculously inappropriate.

I remember conducting a lengthy conversation with my wife about buying stationery in downtown Jerusalem some time in 2001. The number of explosions in the city was such that everyone had instantaneously become an expert suicide bomber. To live one's life one had to be able to guess the obvious locations for the next bomb. Therefore to buy a pad of paper meant evaluating the risks by counting the number of bus stops nearby, the location of other popular shops and cafés, and so on. Bravely confronting the latest perils of Jewish survival I went out onto the front line to do my national duty; to go shopping. Several hours later, paper bought, I could feel satisfaction at having won. In the absurd closeness of the Jerusalem streets as a site of Jewish history, what is the meaning of the Saskatchewan wilderness as a place for feeling 'as if we were there'? On the other hand, why should Jack Kleinman be any different to any other Jew in history who has yearned for Jerusalem, combining both empathy and imagination?

I admire Jack Kleinman for this very reason – space is no barrier to his Jewish journey of the mind, transcending time and space to connect him from out of the wilderness.

Into the Wilderness II: Journey to the Hebrides, Scotland

In spite of the vastness of the Canadian prairies, there are still pockets of Jewish life and culture such as in Hirsch. Yet to fully comprehend the impact of space, one must also consider those places where no such pockets of recognition and comprehension exist.

As a teenager, I went hill walking with school friends on the West Coast of Scotland. Sitting in the common room of a crowded youth hostel in the small village of Uig on a Thursday afternoon with my non-Jewish walking companions, I delivered a short treatise on the nature of the Jewish Sabbath in order to explain why I would be leaving them the next day to spend *Shabbat* away from them in the more appropriate surroundings of Lochmaddy on the outer Hebridean island of North Uist. Lochmaddy, I explained, would be more peaceful and spiritual than the noisy metropolis of Uig, with its three streets and four pubs. Needless to say, they all nodded their supportive, albeit somewhat baffled approval, and asked no particular questions. I sailed off the next morning to North Uist, my soul prepared for a deep and meaningful experience alone with the metaphorical Sabbath bride. It rained all day on that Sabbath, as I believe it does most of the time on North Uist. Spiritual experiences on windswept North Atlantic shores maybe the heroic expectations of early Christian missionaries but not, as I discovered, for middle class seventeen-year-olds from Stanmore with overly active and precocious spiritual aspirations. The Sabbath bride had clearly missed the last crossing and had, more than likely, gone to a kosher resort in Italy for the summer. Wet through to my physical and spiritual core, it became abundantly clear that the beauty of the Jewish Sabbath was not to be found in splendid isolation alone with God and divine creation (the rain and the cold).

The Jewish journey to find God in a beautiful but lonely wilderness revealed quite the opposite of what had been expected. Namely, that the essence of Sabbath lies in the community experience, to be in the world and not out of it. Wildernesses are classic environments for confirming the power of place. The distances are extreme, the environment is often rougher and the overwhelming impact is that of vastness, feeling alone compared to the familiarity of cities. It should not be that surprising to discover that religions are formed by those who have been in the wilderness and come to the city to preach the new truth. My discovery, learnt on a desolate beach and confirmed in the warmth of the ship's canteen as it made its way back to the 'busy' environment of Uig, was that Judaism needs people in families and communities for its magic to work, no less than the secluded grandeur of wildernesses.

Poland

Such personal journeys aside, the field of Jewish education has certainly been a good environment through which to observe others and their journeys. Strangely, two symbolic polarities serve as primary destinations for young and old, namely Israel and Poland. Parents anxious to ensure the continued Jewish identity of their offspring enthusiastically pack them off to Israel in their late teenage years to imbue the holistic Jewish atmosphere of the Jewish state. At the same time Poland, as a site of recent Jewish death, has become no less exciting a location for such potential epiphanies. Therefore the ultimate are those programmes which combine the two locations to create an overpowering and intoxicating environment in which to form identity. Encountering graduates of such programmes provides an intriguing insight into what such journeys do to a person, especially adolescents still forming their identities.

One such graduate was Amy, a bright and effervescent seventeen-year-old from New Jersey who participated on a programme where I was teaching in the mid-1990s. Despite the heat of an Israeli summer, for much of the programme Amy clung tenaciously to a bag containing a blue rain jacket that was occasionally brought out for public show. I confess to having been slightly puzzled at the need for such a garment when the chances of rain were minimal, but all was eventually explained. The programme where we met was devoted to the subject of Jewish leadership, yet somehow it seemed that whenever Amy spoke, it was of the Holocaust. Somehow, in a discussion of Hasidic leadership in eighteenth-century Poland, Amy managed to talk about the Holocaust. When the subject was contemporary Diaspora Jewish leaders, Amy was back in the Holocaust. Unbelievably, at a poolside service to mark the end of the Sabbath, Amy read a poem linked to the Holocaust.

As a teacher inculcated with liberal principles of education I thought it best to wait until she was comfortable with the environment before confronting her with my observation, and sure enough the moment came as we prepared to leave for an excursion to Jerusalem. With great drama and still clutching her blue jacket, Amy took the microphone and announced to all, many of whom were eating their packed lunches already, that this would be an emotional day for her since the last time she had made the 'pilgrimage to Jerusalem', it had been on 'March of the Living', the now-famed programme that brings young Jews to Poland and Israel. She would, as she explained, be wearing the blue jacket she had received on 'the March', the jacket she had worn in Auschwitz. Anyone who has been in certain areas of Poland around Holocaust Remembrance Day would have noticed the hordes of blue-coated young Jews who participate in this programme, the climax of which is a ceremonial walk from Auschwitz I to the site of Auschwitz-Birkenau, where the gas chambers were situated.

To the untrained anthropologist such as myself this type of behaviour was more than intriguing since Amy appeared a well-adjusted and bubbly teenager not unlike her peers. She had many friends, even though there appeared to be a special unspoken bond with four other participants who had also been on 'the March'. They, however, did not carry their blue jackets with them. Amy's boyfriend (who by the end of the programme no longer bore that title after foolishly leaving her blue jacket on a bus!) was a fellow 'March' participant. With so much outwardly normal 'North American Jewish woman' about her, why the Holocaust obsession and why the dramatic donning of a blue jacket in the middle of an Israeli summer?

The conversation on the way to Jerusalem revealed that the journey to Poland six months earlier had been a life-changing moment for Amy, where the bitter truths of Jewish history had been revealed via the forest memorials erected outside former *shtetlech* and the piles of human hair stored behind glass in the Auschwitz museum. Many of the deeper or life-affirming aspects of the Polish Jewish story had clearly been lost in these experiences and what remained was a fixation on the years 1939–45. The link with her

Jewish past had been created and cemented in Poland where she had felt close to where the Jewish People came from. 'My journey to Poland', declared Amy 'changed me forever.'

For better or for worse, Poland and all Holocaust sites have a distinct quality. The historical event is so overwhelming and all-consuming that it seems to work a kind of mysterious power that other places cannot. Some years ago I spent a weekend in Warsaw awaiting the arrival of a group I was to guide the following week. Sitting in the Nozyk synagogue on the Sabbath morning, I placed myself next to a religious Israeli youth who was in Poland with a school group. That group made up 90 per cent of the congregation that Saturday. Half way through the prayers, there was a commotion as a group of secular Israeli high school students arrived with their guide, keen to look at the synagogue, although in their case as an historical site and not a functioning religious location whose service was in full swing. In style not uncharacteristic of the Israeli, they were not that bothered about the fact they were interrupting. At one key moment, a seventeen-year-old boy from the newly-arrived group stopped by my pew and turning the music from his headphones off, he looked at his counterpart from Israel who was until that point deep in prayer. Eyeball to eyeball, these two Israelis youths looked hard at one another. Breaking the silence, one of them, I cannot recall which, uttered the same word as my gym friends had said at Wannsee.

'*Ma ata ose po?*' ('What are you doing here?')

Everything and anything could have been implied in those few words. Somehow, at that moment it became clear that a Jewish journey had succeeded in bringing two Jewish youths some 1,500 kilometres from home to confront their ignorance of the other. Why that meeting was not possible at home seems baffling but nevertheless it seemed a near perfect case of the journey shining a powerful and burning light on the ultimate destination; home. It was a revelation, if not for them, certainly for me, recognizing the sad reality that it takes a journey to Poland, a place so bound up with images of death to discover commonality with fellow citizens.

Confessions of a Parochial Tour Guide: York, Kiev and Rome

The following signpost stands in York, at the foot of the mound leading up to Clifford's Tower. It reads,

> *Clifford's Tower*
> > *The great tower of York Castle*
> > *Built by Henry III*
> *Scene of massacre of Jews in 1190*
> *Panoramic views of the city*
> *Gifts*

I like that sign. It acknowledges that there is more than one way to see the world, or at least York. One day I would like to stand by that sign and interview all those who read it — which of those attractions grabs you? The panoramic views of the city? The castle built by a long-forgotten king? The site of the Jewish massacre or the gifts? It reminds me of a similar tourist artifact that I recently discovered in Krakow; a leaflet advertising the services of a tour company,

Auschwitz-Birkenau
Wieliczka Salt Mine
Rafting
Jazz Music Concert

Well, there is a challenge if ever one was needed. Who could possibly choose between rafting and visiting a death camp? I wonder if they can both be done in the same day? Would lunch be provided? But of course tourism is not that straightforward, since not all experiences are equal and not all pairs of eyes see the same thing. Maybe these signposts and brochures assume that everyone wants to, or at least should want to, consume everything? In which case, I must take issue with the conventions of early twenty-first century tourism and the assumptions that lie behind it.

Frankly, it is not always easy being a committed Jewish traveller in the mind of cosmopolitan and postmodern world of a middle class Western-thinking Israeli. At least not without being accused of narrow-mindedness. On more than one occasion the joking 'comment cum accusation' has been made, that Jewish travel is just another expression of a parochial, inward-looking and self-obsessed view of life. Put another way, to travel with Jewish eyes is regarded by some as an exercise in not seeing the full beauty around. It is to offend against the perceived absolute value of being part of the world, appreciating all manifestations of its cultural bounty and seamlessly moving between identities to be a truly cosmopolitan person. In fact, in Israel of all places, it was argued by some that the whole purpose of the Jewish national project was to enable such a cosmopolitan Jew to emerge since Jews would no longer feel defensive about their position in the world. They would be less insecure, less close minded and more able to enjoy the world in all its diversity. This being the case, I recognize myself to have only achieved this half of this exalted aspiration. I am an uneven and inconsistent cosmopolitan, interested in many aspects of the world but nevertheless burdened with only one set of eyes.

In his novel *The Fixer*, Bernard Malamud feeds one of his protagonists the following line about the Ukrainian capital of Kiev:

> ... but what I don't understand is why you
> want to bother with Kiev. It's a dangerous
> city full of Churches and anti-Semites.[?]

I must confess to liking that line because it both
reflects my own experience of the city and it affirms
the right to have a parochial view of the world. Kiev
may be magnificent for some and fascinating for
others, but to me it ranks in the top ten most successful locations for Jew hatred. A one-sided view of
travel? Maybe, but what can I do? These are my eyes
and that is Kiev.

Standing at the centre of the city I encountered
a large statue of the seventeenth-century Ukrainian
hero, Bogdan Chmielnicki. In addition to his
undoubted credentials as warrior hetman and defender
of the Ukrainian people, his reputation amongst Jews
is somewhat different to say the least. In fact he is
right up there in the pantheon of great Jew haters of
history, having murdered more than 50,000 Jews in
the years 1648–9. But the past is the past, shout the
'open minded'. Yes, reply the 'closed minded', but

57

why the statue? Try as I might to be open-minded and see the whole Kiev, I struggled with the city for that very reason, all of its beauty notwithstanding. I endeavored to put collective memory in my back pocket until a sufficiency of Ukrainian beauty had been enjoyed. Later I crossed the road only to find myself by the court room where the notorious Mendel Beillis trial was held in 1913. Beillis was the supervisor at a local brick kiln who found himself arrested and standing trial on the medieval charge of ritual murder. It took a supreme effort led by international Jewish bodies before he was released. Then again, the accusers were Tsarist officials and not the good people of Kiev and so there could still be room for enjoying the city once more. Yet by the time I reached Babi Yar all pretence was over. With a fair degree of local assistance, the Nazis managed to kill just over 33,000 Jews on one weekend at the end of September 1941.

Let me be clear; Kiev is indeed a beautiful and fascinating city. St. Sophia Cathedral on the sought side of Sofiyska plosshcha is a mysterious and entrancing edifice, combining Byzantine systems of decoration with later Eastern Slavic Orthodox stylistic forms. By way of contrast the city also boasts the ornate Shevchenko Opera and Ballet Theatre, a testament to the development of modern Ukrainian national culture in the nineteenth century. Beyond these physical sites, the city represents a captivating story of modern nationalism in the context of the ever-complex world of Slavic identity. Yet it was still hard to really enjoy myself. The stains on the cityscape were just too obvious to ignore and the images of persecution just too evident. In fact I found myself retreating to the warmth of the late nineteenth-century synagogue building in Podol which has survived pogrom and massacre yet remains a functioning community centre. I genuinely tried to maintain a cosmopolitan outlook in Kiev but all it showed me was the limitations of that world view.

My real answer to the advocates of cosmopolitan travel is to suggest a different framework for the discussion. Perhaps tourism should be acknowledged as a more reflective experience, inviting tourists to see themselves through the sites of others. If the buildings and monuments of others are the expression of their cultures, then our observations of them must come in the form of dialogue in which sites speak their language, tourists offer their reactions and wherever possible all join together to develop the conversation.

It has always been my wish to halt the tourist daily proceedings by the Arch of Titus in Rome. On any given day of the year, guides can be found by the famous arch, explaining in all languages that it was built by Titus' brother, Domitian, after the emperor's death in CE 81 to commemorate his victories in Judea eleven years earlier. If I had my way, we would allow these facts to be explained and then invite all who wished to consider a different point of view. The arch is the ultimate symbol of Jewish defeat, of the loss of sovereignty and the experience of exile. Titus destroyed the Temple in Jerusalem, triggering off a great theological crisis for Judaism and providing proof for Christianity of God's rejection of His covenant with the Jews. He also brought Jewish captives to Rome as slaves, consigning them to a life of wandering for hundreds of years. Then again, I would also have to point out, that on 14 May 1948, following the decision by the United Nations the previous November, a Jewish State was proclaimed in that same land. On that very same day, the Chief Rabbi of Rome assembled the Jewish community and led them in a symbolic walk backwards through the Arch of Titus, signifying the end of that cycle of history. Finally, since the temptation would be too great, I would point to the remains of the Roman Forum and the Palatine and remind the listening tourists that the Jews have outlived the Roman Empire!

But what of the dialogue? My story told, I envisage fantastic conversations between people of many cultures and experiences regarding questions of exile, power, empires, memory and history. If it was all going well, we could move on to the other sites of Rome. I would love to ask them what they make of Rome's obsession with size. Whatever the Imperial Forums may have been to the ancient world, what does one say about the not-insubstantial size of St. Peter's Square and Basilica, the rich and exquisite beauty of the Sistine Chapel and the monumental grandeur of the Vittorio Emanuele monument that celebrates the modern Italian nation through endless piles of white marble? Are these entirely necessary or are they merely an expression of the insecurity of those in power? The dialogue would then begin.

As a Jewish traveller I would find it hard to be quiet! For a start, Jewish building has always been small but mainly because others have decreed it that way. In the Rome ghetto, Jews were only permitted one small synagogue, cramming five different communities into one structure which was anything but big. But since emancipation they too have built a stunning and richly decorated building. Elsewhere in Europe, since the onset of modernity and integration of Jews into society, other Jewish communities have also got a bit carried away. But the core point would be that the Jewish equivalent is the power of the written word and not the bricks and mortar of buildings. What else are buildings than the expression of deeper aspirations to be seen in the world? What is a synagogue building when compared to a stack of Hebrew books for a form of self-expression? And I can't think of a better way to appreciate St. Peter's Basilica than to stand within it, discuss with others how one reaches the divine and how else one builds a temple to glory. Or to stand on the triumphal temple of modern nationalism and consider the true meaning of power and sovereignty.

Returning to York, Clifford's Tower and its intriguing signposts, it turned out that the tourist potential was none of those advertised, but rather an opportunity for one such dialogue. I was standing with a colleague in the windy exposed courtyard of Clifford's Tower, wondering if we were at the very spot where, in 1190, Rabbi Yom Tov of Joigny called on the Jewish community who were holed up there to commit suicide rather than be forcibly baptised by the seething mob outside. A man placed his hand on my shoulder and asked in the politest way possible, 'Excuse me for asking, but are you a real Jew?'.

I confessed and we had a brief conversation in which he explained how he had always admired 'your people' and was now glad to have now met a real living example. Keen to return the enthusiasm I asked him where he was from, to which he explained Liverpool, but originally Ireland. Then he added, I assume in reference to the site, 'We've also had our fair share of suffering, not like you people of course …'. So there it was, standing at the top of Clifford's Tower, surrounded by panoramic views of the city, the site of a Jewish massacre and a gift shop, an Irishman confessed to a Jew who he was and acknowledged our common experience of suffering. I admit I had gone there for my own parochial reasons and I suspect he had too, but in so doing we discovered each other.

Personal Jewish Journey

The professional demands of being a guide, the person who tries to validate and activate the sorts of experiences described here, is to acknowledge that people are on journeys and not merely travelling to places. For that very reason, there can be no guiding of others without being aware of one's own journey.

In the year before my father died, everything was a journey. I was researching a travel book at the same time as trying to visit him *en route* to Israel from the Jewish cities of Europe. It was then I became aware of the complex meaning of 'journey', both as a metaphor and as a real, lived experience. Leaving home each month meant interrupting family life in order to find inspiration in the Jewish quarters of Italy, Spain, Germany and beyond. It meant having to think across time periods, attempting to identify with the dilemmas of communities in different centuries. The literature to be read on planes, trains, trams and buses was anything that would make the sites come alive. Buoyed by the thrill of discovery and potential success, I would stop off in London in the hope of finding my parents in good spirits and encouraged by positive news from the doctors. Invariably this was not forthcoming and the stop-offs between thrilling research and the loving embrace of the family in Jerusalem became a journey of a different type.

In healthier times, the rituals of family visiting had always involved my father picking me up or dropping me off at the airport. For all the sadness of living away from my parents, I think they were pleased with my decision to live in Israel, representing a type of success for their values. So the airport became a sort of metaphor for Jewish history, the point of transition between the Land of Israel and the Diaspora. The thought was reinforced when I flew back in the days before he died. I remember being troubled by the question of what to pack for such a journey. Having ceased the rituals of daily prayer some years earlier, I felt mildly guilty packing my prayer book, *tallit* (prayer shawl) and *tefillin* (phylacteries) since I knew that I would need them for the *shiva* (seven-day mourning period). In all my fluster the one item I forgot was a bag of earth from the Land of Israel, to be placed in his coffin as some traditions dictate. It was one last chance to affirm the great journey of Jewish history, by bringing a piece of the land that I had rooted myself in, to the private world of his resting-place.

Looking back, those were both intensely personal and intensely Jewish journeys, fusing together the powerful forces of the small, lived world of family and the large, amorphous world of Jewish history and destiny.

Context:
The Idea of Journey in Jewish Experience

It is said that the famous Marxist historian Isaac Deutscher, a Jewish refugee from 1930s Poland, was pestered in a Cambridge university common room by a colleague who insisted on discussing the issue of his Jewish roots. Irritated, Deutscher retorted, 'Trees have roots, Jews have legs!'.

There is a wonderful ambiguity in Deutscher's outburst since it is not clear whether he was simply evaluating history or making a statement of intrinsic nature. Have Jews been forced to be wanderers or do they find this more creative and satisfying? Similarly, are they against setting down roots or has the desire to have permanent places always been interrupted by forces beyond their control?

The Jewish People have been formed on journeys,

from early Biblical wanderings until the present day. There is hardly a single achievement in Jewish history that has not been related to the journey across land or sea. On a simple yet fundamental level, the central Jewish book, the Torah, complete with its ethical and moral codes, was created as the Jews were on the move from Egypt to Israel. Even when they arrived in their own land, the Jews insisted on making journeys to a central shrine to express who they were and communicate with their God. They elevated the epic of desert wandering to a hallowed status by inserting its remembrance into almost every celebration and practice.

On the deeper level, there are variant expressions of wandering: journeys with a fixed point of destination (e.g. the Exodus from Egypt); those without (e.g. the expulsion from Spain); journeys of choice (e.g. Benjamin of Tudela's remarkable twelfth-century travels across the Jewish world); journeys of compulsion (e.g. fleeing persecution and economic hardship); journeys defined by their context (Exile as Divine punishment); journeys defined by a searching for something (e.g. contemporary 'pilgrimages' to Poland, searching for a lost world); collective journeys (mass emigrations); and all the endless journeys of the individual. Throughout, there is a consistent tension between the physical and the spiritual dimension of the journey, a reflection of the same drama that defines the meaning of being Jewish.

Naturally, a central pivot of the Jewish journey has been the relationship with the Land of Israel, the one core value that would seem to support the 'roots not legs' position. Yet, to a degree the *de facto* Jewish relationship with its land has been based on movement, going towards and away from it – having wandered for 40 years to arrive there, just over 600 years later they were sitting by the waters of Babylon lamenting it. For hundred of years in the Middle Ages, the rituals of remembrance were central to Jewish memory, yet few chose or were able to physically go there. The journey remained in the imagination. In modern times, after all the travails of the Jewish People in the last hundred years, the Jews remain in a complex relationship with their land. Roughly 50 per cent live in it, many have never visited it, yet it appears to be uppermost in their minds. This would suggest that, for better or for worse, Jews display a desire to be in a 'journey relationship' with the Land of Israel, both there and not there at the same time.

The parallel 'homeland' experience has been the phenomenon of culture. Fundamental to Jewish life is its portable 'homeland', the endless creating and regenerating repository of ideas, known as the 'the text', which has evolved through the long years of journeying. Physically this intellectual, legal and spiritual storehouse has been created, making it a powerful testament to the role of geography in the creation of culture. The Talmud, for instance, the central text for defining Jewish life, was created in Babylon and Palestine then studied simultaneously in Cordoba, Worms and Baghdad, all before the invention of the printing press. When the text could be mass-produced the process only became more sophisticated, to the point that the most important digest of Jewish law, the *Shulchan Aruch*, was to be written by two rabbis, one in the Land of Israel and the other in Poland in the sixteenth century in relation to each other. Without these texts there would be no Judaism, and yet both were created across continents. The Jewish text was born and matured through the endless journeys of people, ideas, commentary, knowledge and insight across the Jewish world.

The centrality of the journey to Jewish life is a broad claim, and one that demands greater elaboration. What then are the components of those journeys and what are the main journeys of Jewish history?

Components of the Jewish Journey
Physical Journeys, Spiritual Journeys
With dramatic flourish as well as slight literary ambiguity, the Jewish journey is launched in the early chapters of the Bible. As if from nowhere, the Biblical text suddenly speaks of a person who will apparently become the first Jew and to whom the following command is given, '*Vayomer Adonai el-Avram lech lecha m'artzcha u'mimoladtcha u'mibeit avicha el-ha'aretz asher areicha*', 'Now the Lord said to Abram, Get thee out of thy country, and from thy kindred and

from they father's house, to the land that I will show thee'. Conventional translations from the King James Bible onwards have all adopted the meaning of the Hebrew command, '*lech lecha*' to mean 'get thee out'. Yet literally the phrase has a far richer, more subtle meaning than simply to 'get out'. An alternative rendering of the text would have the phrase meaning 'go to yourself', a complicated notion suggesting the journey was not outward at all but inwards. By leaving the land of his birth and his father's house, the soon-to-be father of a new nation was in fact drawing closer to his own inner self. In similar terms, the great nineteenth century commentator, R. Jacob Zvi Mecklenburg (1785–1865), known in Hebrew as *Haketav V'hakabala*, points out in his commentary on the Torah that one would have expected the text to have a different order for Abram's departure; leaving his home first followed by the place of his birth and then his country. Instead, the emphasis is placed on his final location, that of his father's home, since departure from there represented the greatest emotional and spiritual break. *Haketav V'hakabala* concluded that this was a spiritual journey and not merely a physical one. Such was the power of the journey that his name would eventually be changed and Abraham would emerge, a man dedicated to his notion of a single God, morality and the centrality of human life. The first Jewish journey thus blurred the boundaries between the outer and the inner self.

Armed with mission and purpose, Abram's journey was to serve as a metaphor for many subsequent travels undertaken by Jews through their long history. His was a journey into the unknown where only the point of origin was clear. Faith was the sustaining force which would eventually carry him to a place that would become 'sacred'. Indeed, it was this journey that first established a connection for Jews with the Land of Israel, the pivot around which Jewish geography would locate itself. Would that we could interview the nomad Abram about his confidence that this would end well and that the place God would show him would not turn out to be a mere illusion. The 'place' after all was no more than an idea, a symbol, or a means through which greater things could be achieved. Was he worried? How did he picture this place? Was there recognition that the reality would never match the dream? Or maybe he was one of those special types of travellers for whom imagination and belief was sufficient? One thing seems clear, he rarely appears settled and is constantly moving: coming to Canaan, going down to Egypt, going south, to Beer Sheba, to Sodom and Gomorrah, to Jerusalem to sacrifice his son and then to Hebron to bury his wife. Each journey and each new location brought opportunities for him to present his vision. To signify the change, his name was changed from Abram to Abraham. Quite apart from the negative connotations the term would generate in later Christian theology, Abraham is an intriguing prototype of 'the wandering Jew'.

From Abraham's story of the lone wanderer would come the epic Jewish adventure of all time, namely the Exodus from Egyptian bondage and subsequent journey through the wilderness. Unlike Abram, the Exodus from Egypt was for an entire nation, twelve tribes-worth of Israelites who had endured common suffering at the hands of the Pharaoh. The departure would enter Jewish consciousness as a momentous occasion, with the full force of God's power expressed through nature. Plagues were brought down on the Egyptians, there were pillars of cloud and fire to lead them and eventually the sea would part to allow them safe escape from their pursuers. This was a journey never to be repeated, a witness to God's entry onto the stage of earthly history, described by the Torah as a 'night of watching'.[1] Indeed, even before their departure, the leader Moses had elevated the journey to the level of founding myth for the nation.

> And Moses said to the people, 'Remember
> this day, on which you went free from
> Egypt, the house of bondage, how the Lord
> freed you from it with a mighty hand …
> And you shall explain to your son on that
> day, "It is because that which the Lord did
> for me when I went free from Egypt."'.[2]

Only once the future memory of the Exodus has been established does the Torah relate the journey.

> And it came to pass, when Pharaoh had
> let the people go, that God led them not
> by the way of the land of the Philistines
> although that was near; for God said: In
> case the people change their minds when
> they see war and they return to Egypt. But
> God led the people about, by the way of
> the wilderness, by the Red Sea; and the
> children of Israel went up armed out of the
> land of Egypt. And Moses took the bones of
> Joseph with him; for he had promised the
> children of Israel, saying "God will surely
> remember you and you shall carry my bones
> with you". And they took the journey from
> Succot and encamped at Etham in the edge
> of the wilderness. And the Lord went before
> them by day in a pillar of cloud, to lead
> them the way, and by night in a pillar of
> fire, to give them light …[3]

Several elements define this journey: the route was designed to strengthen them, avoiding the possibility of returning to slavery; previous generations were present through the insistence of taking the bones of Joseph (it was he after all who had brought the Israelites to Egypt in the first place); and finally, God accompanied them suggesting that like Abram's *lech lecha*, this was a journey of the spirit too.

One intriguing aspect of this journey was the route, since without the stops and circuitous path there would have been no need to remain in the wilderness for the next 40 years. If it took just one night to leave, why did it take so long to arrive? Having left with such noise and drama, one imagines the Israelites overwhelmed by the deafening silence of the desert and asking 'what next?' All is explained seven weeks later as they gathered at foot of Mount Sinai to receive the Torah and chain themselves to its precepts. The epic journey would not be complete until a new culture was created, complete with laws of ethical, moral and ritual conduct necessary to function as truly free people. The Torah, received at this transitional stage of the journey, provides a link with the destination, the Land of Israel. With another 39 years until they arrived, the Israelites, the 'proto-Jews', needed time to learn how to control their own destiny. It was this journey as a people alone in the wilderness that created them. During this time, the entire generation of slaves would die out before a new generation would arise to face the challenge of freedom.

The setting for the journey was the wilderness, the desert, a transitional space where the unruly slaves become a disciplined and God-fearing nation. There are etymological clues to the meaning of the wilderness journey in the root of the Hebrew word for desert, *midbar,* coming as it does from the verb *daber* meaning to speak. What better description could there be for such a Jewish journey, where the environment spoke and the people responded? Having left physical slavery on their way to adopting a monotheistic and legal culture, the Jews needed to travel through a place of speaking in order to transform themselves.

To return to the earlier claim that the Jewish People

were born on a journey, the legacy of this moment in Jewish history was written into the culture of rituals and performance. There was to be a re-telling of the journey, in the form of the annual *seder* service to be held on the first night of Passover, complete with rituals of re-enactment, prayers, study, discussion and of course food. The text for the evening, the *Hagadah*, reads

> In every generation it is incumbent
> on every person to imagine that they
> personally had departed from Egypt.

How precisely one imagines being personally on a journey that took place thousands of years ago is a matter for discussion, but there can be no mistaking the intention here, namely to continue the sense of the journey. It is the tradition amongst various Jews of North African and Middle Eastern descent to don the ragged clothes of slaves for the night of Passover and at various stages of the ceremony to walk literally around the table, in some cases even walking over a bowl of water to symbolize the Red Sea. Beyond the annual re-enactment, Jewish culture has evolved other moments for recalling its epic foundation journey. Every week for at least the last 1,500 years, the prayers that sanctify the weekly Sabbath have included the phrase '*zecher l'yztiat mitzrayim*', 'in remembrance of the Exodus from Egypt'. The Sabbath, the enforced weekly period of rest designed to mimic God's resting from the act of creation, the affirmation of life as a free human being is somehow linked to the historical journey to freedom. Whether still on a journey or settled, at a place of 'home' or still wandering, this is a fixed moment to be reminded of the journey across the desert from slavery to freedom and its significance.

These two stories, Abraham and the Exodus, provide symbolic starting-points for understanding the broader idea of Jewish journeys and the role they play in Jewish life. They are original myths, the founding stories that the nation uses to speak of itself. However, by necessity they must be set against the broader story of Jewish travel, the actual journeys undertaken by Jews through their history. These include everything: from the harvest pilgrimages during ancient times to the journeys of Babylonian and Roman exile; from the wanderings of the Diaspora/Exile to the modern return of Jews to the Land of Israel. Before analyzing these some consideration should be given to one simple question, what defines a Jewish journey?

Places

To speak of journeys and travel is to talk about places and the concept of 'place' itself. Tourists and travellers in general relate to the destinations of their travels in different ways. For the conventional holidaymaker the destination has utilitarian value, to be a place for escape and to forget about home. These travellers do not necessarily project meaning or deep value on to the places they go. For 'cultural tourists' on the other hand, the destination is critical, providing the *raison d'être* for the trip. Renaissance art lovers must therefore go to Florence, enthusiastic climbers must go to the Himalayas and wine connoisseurs to whichever region is currently in vogue. Then there are the pilgrims for whom there is only one destination namely the sacred sites that transform them and make them whole.

In all these examples, the traveller is challenged to define the level of affinity they have with their destination. Are they just enjoying themselves, experiencing and experimenting with the values and culture of the destination, or are they elevating it to a place of existential value? The issue is complicated further when the normative culture of the traveller intrudes providing value judgments regarding these destinations. In traditional Western terms, something tells the tourist to value the Sistine Chapel as a place of high cultural value, quite beyond the religious intentions of those who commissioned Michelangelo to paint it. Similar judgments are made with visits to the Houses of Parliament (mother of democracy), the Acropolis (ancient civilization) or First World War cemeteries (modern history). In short, there is a relationship between traveller and society on the one hand, and the place and its story on the other, that collectively define the value of the journey.

How does this work for Jewish journeys?

Unlike Islam and much of Christianity, Judaism does not have a strong notion of pilgrimage, i.e. journeys to specific locations for the purpose of religious fulfillment. The only parallel was in ancient times, when Israelites were required to bring sacrifices of their first fruits to the Temple (see below). In other words, Judaism struggles with the idea of sacredness in relation to journeys, with few places deserving of veneration. In more contemporary times this has changed slightly as Jewish travellers have begun to elevate certain historical memory sites (e.g. death camps) as locations for modern-day pilgrimages, but this is not yet a mass phenomenon. It all leads to the conclusion that in strictly religious terms, Judaism is lacking a strong pilgrimage tradition. This is ironic given the prominence of journeys in Jewish experience.

In very broad terms, Jewish tradition demarcates two places, the Land of Israel and everywhere else, which is, admittedly a rather unsophisticated way of seeing the world! This was re-asserted by modern

Zionists with their vocabulary of national exile and redemption. To understand the Jewish relationship to places, one must therefore grasp the significance of the Land of Israel, since journeys to and from it have a different status to those elsewhere.

The nineteenth-century Hasidic Rabbi Nachman of Bratzlav said 'Wherever I travel, I travel to the Land of Israel'. In poetic fashion, Rabbi Nachman reiterated the age-old notion of the centrality of the Land of Israel in Jewish consciousness. In the domain of poetry, Rabbi Nachman was on safe ground, but the controversy starts if this is turned into theological imperative. Is the Land of Israel considered 'holy' in the transformative sense, whereby one remains 'less than' if one has not visited it? The answer surprisingly enough is no.

The Land of Israel is called various things: 'holy'; 'promised'; 'flowing with milk and honey', etc. In Temple times there were certain rituals and observances that are relevant only to the Land of Israel such as the '*shmittah*' when the land must lie fallow every seventh year; and the '*yovel*' (jubilee) when all land reverts to its previous owners every 50 years to restore freedom and justice. Central to the traditional notion of the land, however, was its conditional value. It was given on the basis of true loyalty to commandments and ethical moral behaviour, and was made holy by the actions of those living on it. Furthermore, the land does not 'belong' to the Jewish People in a religious sense, but to God. This had profound and timeless application in the domain of history since the consequence of failure to live up to the terms of the Covenant was exile, described endlessly by the Hebrew prophets and reconfirmed by the rabbis after it had happened. Only messianic redemption could change that status and this, according to all streams of Judaism, has not occurred yet. Thus the strange situation arises whereby Ultra Orthodox Jews living in contemporary Jerusalem can still refer to themselves as living in Exile. Exiles, like journeys, can be spiritual as well as physical.

The one exception when land was elevated to a higher status was the Temple in ancient times where God's presence was said to dwell. Only members of the priesthood could go to certain places, in particular the Holy of Holies, which today sits under the Dome of the Rock on the Temple Mount. All households were obliged to show their loyalty to God by bringing their sacrifices of first fruits. Interestingly, after the Temple's destruction, the result of this acknowledged sacredness raised the question as to how close could Jews go in walking through the remains of the temple. This continues today with wariness in some quarters about Jews going up as tourists to the Temple Mount in case they should by mistake tread on the site of the Holy of Holies.

Holiness therefore is not abstract magic but one element in the relationship between places and people. As one nineteenth-century commentator describes it,

> Everything that is holy – the Land of
> Israel, Jerusalem, etc. – is no more than
> an aspect of the Torah, and is sanctified
> by the holiness of the Torah ... Do not
> imagine that the temple and the sanctuary

are holy in and of themselves, God forbid!
God dwells amongst His people, and if
they break His covenant, they (the Temple
and the Sanctuary) lose their holiness and
become as profane objects ... The tablets,
bearing the writing of God, are also not
holy in and of themselves ... In sum, there
is nothing holy in the world ... Holiness
exists in no created thing, except insofar
as the people of Israel keeps the Torah in
accordance with the will of the Creator.[4]

The *Meshech Hochmah*, the author of these words, was
not seeking to downplay the relationship of Jews to the
Land of Israel but simply to clarify the question of its
holiness. It would be holy when the people (the Jews)
were themselves holy. Regarding travel and journeys,
no spiritual necessity exists for Jews to visit the land
once the Jews had been exiled, which is one explanation for why so few Jews, relatively speaking, made it
a priority to journey there during the time of exile. At
the same time, Israel and Jerusalem remained rooted

in the consciousness of Jews throughout their history, with whole systems established for remembrance.

All that has been described so far must be seen as separate from the attitude of contemporary Zionism to the Land of Israel. Utilising the language of modern nationalism, sacredness of place was secularized; God and Covenant was replaced by 'destiny' or 'history' to create a powerful desire to journey to the land, to settle it and be at one with it.

Diaspora Places

Away from the holiness of the Land of Israel, Jewish history has produced various areas of secondary specialness with regard to physical space. For the last thousand years, the Jewish world has recognized two domains of cultural-physical space, known as 'Ashkenaz' and 'Sepharad', the former denoting the communities of Central and Eastern Europe, and the latter from the Iberian peninsula. These labels are intriguing since they have outlived the time when Jews actually lived there. This is particularly recognizable amongst Sephardi Jews, who were expelled at the end of the fifteenth century, yet continue to wear the definition as a clear mark of pride and self-affirmation. There are also Italian, Yemenite, Iraqi and Ethiopian Jews whose history (or at least group myths) pre-date the Sephardi–Ashkenazi divide.

Significant though these descriptions of places may be, they do not produce any imperative to visit them. Instead they establish an equally powerful cultural dynamic – identity. Ashkenazi Jews travelling in the Jewish world will always be Ashkenazi Jews, and as such are aware of their own points of origin. Ashkenazi Jews of German origin, however, have evolved different cultural styles to those of Ashkenazim from Poland or Lithuania. Meanwhile between the Polish and Lithuanian Jews there are all manner of religious, intellectual and cultural variant traditions. The Sephardi Jews of Amsterdam were different from those of the Balkans. In practical terms these labels enable the emergence of variant liturgical, linguistic and ritual traditions. The prayers may be the same, for instance, but the pronunciation, melody and style of public performance are markedly different.

The places of Jewish living have asserted themselves in other ways, producing an interesting hierarchy as well as novel ways of describing them. For instance, for hundreds of years the Lithuanian city of Vilna has been known as '*Yerushalayim d' Lita*', the 'Jerusalem of Lithuania', marking it out as a special community. The Jewish community in Lithuania regarded its level of scholarly learning and religious piety as well as cohesiveness as deserving of such an appellation. Similarly, Salonika was known as the 'Jerusalem of the Balkans'. The famous Russian Jewish historian (arguably the greatest) Simon Dubnow built an entire theory of Jewish history around the notion of such great cultural centres, arguing that there has always been a hierarchy of places according to the level of cultural sophistication and achievement. Meanwhile, the idea of Jewish community in general is one that points to a place that is not bound by the borders of physical geography. The standard phrase used to denote such a place is the powerful phrase '*kehilat kodesh*' ('holy community') offering an intriguing commentary on how holiness was transformed when the Temple no longer existed.

Consciousness as Place

Beyond the bi-polar conception of space (Israel and the rest), there is a third place, which is no less powerful and acts as a bridge between all places – consciousness. In one of his last poems, the contemporary Israeli poet Yehuda Amichai wrote the following in his poem, 'Jewish Travel,' which examines the relationship between travel and journey.

> Yehuda Halevi wrote, "In the East is my
>   heart, and I dwell at the end of the
>   West."
> That's Jewish travel, that's the Jewish game
>   of hearts between east and west,
> between self and heart, to and fro, to
>   without fro, fro without to,
> fugitive and vagabond without sin ...[5]

As he describes, Jewish journeys are rarely about 'place' exclusively, but the total experience of moving between zones of experience and being. 'East' is a place of the heart, but 'West' is a place of the body.

The journey encapsulates all parts of a person – body, heart, consciousness ('I', 'self', etc), intellect and emotion. Yet most significantly, all the great travels of Jewish history, from Abraham to Jonah, the Israelites in the wilderness to the wandering Jews of the world, the explorers to the refugees have all been on journeys that brought body and soul together. The relationship between heart and body is a vital one with each affecting the other.

At its most spiritual (and complicated), places are regarded as a reflection of God's creative powers. Of the many names given to God in Jewish literature, a common one in rabbinic and Kabbalistic texts is '*ha-makom*', literally meaning 'the place'. Its purpose is to describe the omnipresence of Divine glory, affirming the idea that as the supreme creator of the physical world, God is in all places. In *midrash* (exegetic and homiletical commentary), God is indeed the place (*makom*) of the universe even though the universe is not His exclusive place. Humans may need places to exist but God extends far beyond, being the ultimate expression of omnipresence and omnipotence. The physical world conceals the spiritual force of creation. God as the creator and power of the world, is thus understood as 'the place'

This leads to one important conclusion, that all places are connected to God and sacredness does not rest in any one place. Humans may attribute extra holiness to a certain space but this does not imply exclusive holiness. Nevertheless, to acknowledge the importance of places is also to come closer to the profound world of God's creation. Based on this, one can imagine a Jewish journey to marvel at the wonders of creation, in nature, in cities or in fact anywhere that one chooses.

Motion/Movement

The last building block of the Jewish journey is the actual notion of journey – 'movement' or 'motion'. Superficially, it may seem trite to discuss the role of movement in relation to journeys, since there is no journey without movement. However, the true question is what type of motion is necessary? The medieval commentator Rashi (1040–1105) offers a fascinating insight in his explanation of a verse in the Book of Exodus which speaks of a cloud that accompanied the Israelites in the wilderness and moved when they did. He points out that the place of encampment seems to be called by the same word for journey (*masa*). Why is this so? Because from the place of encampment they always set out again on a new journey, therefore all the elements of the journey, the stationary encampments and the physical motion are both known as '*masa'ot*' ('journeys', plural of *masa*). Here lies a first indicator for appreciating the meaning of Jewish journey, that despite being physically stationary, movement is taking place on a higher level.

The same issue occurs in a Talmudic discussion between two rabbis regarding the correct manner for reciting the prayer for a journey. The matter under discussion is whether the words are to be said standing still or whilst actually on the journey. Both are permissible, although moving is preferred, but the inference is that journeys are not entirely about physical motion. One can be 'on a journey' even though one is standing still. The discussion in this section of the Talmud continues on a topic that outwardly appears to be unconnected but in actual fact is very much related, namely the direction for prayer.

> If one is standing outside Palestine,
> he should turn mentally towards *Eretz
> Yisrael* (the Land of Israel) ... If he stands
> in *Eretz Yisrael* he should turn mentally
> towards Jerusalem ... If he is standing
> in Jerusalem he should turn mentally
> towards the Sanctuary ... If he is standing
> in the Sanctuary, he should turn mentally
> towards the Holy of Holies ... If he was
> standing in the Holy of Holies he should
> turn mentally towards the mercy-seat ...
> If he was standing behind the mercy-seat,
> he should imagine himself to be in front
> of the mercy-seat. Consequently, if he is in
> the east he should turn his face to the west;
> if in the west he should turn his face to the
> east; if in the south he should turn his face

to the north; if in the north he should turn his face to the south. In this way all Israel will be turning their hearts towards one place.[6]

In short, there are places where one can be without actually being there.

Journeys of the Jews

Dissecting its component parts is one path to understanding the nature of the Jewish journey. Another is to describe the journeys themselves.

Aliya b' Regel /Pilgrimage

Within the drama of the Biblical Israelites and their journeys, a new reality dawned once they put slavery and the wilderness behind them and settled down to face the challenge of living out the terms of their Covenant with God in the Land of Israel. What then became of the 'journey'? In this setting an intriguing new ritual was born (Exodus 23:17; 34: 23, Deuteronomy 16:16; 26), whereby the life of wandering was transformed into a ritual of re-enactment. Three times a year the Israelites were to bring their first fruits, the symbol of renewal and God's commitment to continued life, and carry them on a journey of sacrifice. This was where the idea of pilgrimage entered Jewish tradition. For the Israelite farmer, this was a journey of necessity since without the contact with God that pilgrimage allowed, his future fortunes could not be guaranteed.

At first the journey led them to the sanctuary and later, once it was built by King Solomon, to the Temple in Jerusalem. Critically, in terms of the evolution of Israelite culture and memory, it was during this time that the three harvest festivals of the year were transformed into commemorations of the Exodus and the journey through the wilderness. All journeys thus became interconnected, the Exodus from Egypt, the entry to the land and ultimately the pilgrimage.

Regarding the rituals of the journey itself, the Torah is quite precise. A formula of words was chosen that is both fascinating and challenging in order to understand what was took place.

The priest shall take the basket from your hands and set it down in front of the altar of the Lord your God. Then you shall declare before the Lord your God. "My father was a wandering Aramean, and he went down into Egypt with a few people and lived there and became a great nation, powerful and numerous. But the Egyptians mistreated us and made us suffer, and they gave to us hard labour. Then we cried out to the Lord, the God of our fathers, and the Lord heard our voice and saw our misery, toil and oppression. So the Lord brought us out of Egypt with a mighty hand and an outstretched arm, with great terror and with miraculous signs and wonders. He brought us to this place and gave us this land, a land flowing with milk and honey; and now I bring the first fruits of the soil that you, O Lord, have given me."[7]

This speech was the pivotal moment of the pilgrimage as the produce was handed over to God. The Israelite made his own declaration, linking him to all the journeys of the Israelites so far, from wanderer to redeemed and settled people. It is all the more remarkable if one considers that the rabbis of the Talmud chose this very speech as the central section of the *seder* night service on Passover. Sitting down to their annual retelling of the Exodus story complete with its re-enactment rituals, this was a grand revisiting of the journeys of the nation. In the long years of exile, when there was no Temple sacrifice, the recitation of the speech was a reminder of a journey that would one day in the future be restored.

'Exile', 'Home'

The Jewish journey concept could never remain static since the forces of history constantly created a new Jewish geography. Original responses were needed to explain the changed relationship to places and to lay out new rituals for remembrance. In 586 BCE, the Babylonians under Nebuchadnezzar conquered the Land of Israel, destroyed the temple in Jerusalem and carried away a significant section of the population to Babylon as exiles. For the first time, there was a significant group journey in the opposite direction, a forced journey at that, away from the Land of Israel and away from the central shrine. It seemed as if the very nature of Israelite culture and identity was threatened. How could the Jews communicate with their God if they no longer had a sacred temple to offer sacrifices? The pain and anguish is captured by the psalmist in a very distinct type of Jewish travel literature.

> By the rivers of Babylon, there we sat, sat and
>   wept as we remembered Zion,
> There on the willows we hung up our lyres,
> for our captors asked us there for songs, our
>   tormentors, for amusement,
> "Sing us one of the songs of Zion."
> How can we sing a song of the Lord on alien soil?
> If I forget you, O Jerusalem, let my right hand wither;
> let my tongue stick to my palate if I cease to
>   think of you,

if I do not keep Jerusalem in memory even at my
*   happiest hour.*
Remember, O Lord, against the Edomites the day
*   of Jerusalem's fall;*
how they cried, "Strip her, strip her to her very
*   foundations!"*
Fair Babylon, you predator,
a blessing on him who repays you in kind what
*   you have inflicted on us;*
a blessing on him who seizes your babies
and dashes them against the rocks.[8]

In these short lines that would become the very
symbol of Jewish yearning for another place, all the
fear and confusion that characterized exile gushes
forth. It offers mournful reflection, nostalgia and
yearning for a place far away, as well as a call for
revenge in the second section and a meditation on
future events. By comparison, it is worth considering
the words of the prophet Jeremiah, written in relation
to a smaller destruction and 'proto-exile' to Babylon
some ten years before.

Now these are the words of the letter that
Jeremiah the prophet sent from Jerusalem
to the residue of the elders who were
carried away captives, and to the priests,
and to the prophets, and to all the people
whom Nebuchadnezzar had carried away
captive from Jerusalem to Babylon ...
"Thus says the Lord of hosts, the God of
Israel, to all that are carried away captives,
whom I have caused to be carried away
from Jerusalem to Babylon; Build houses,
and dwell in them; and plant gardens,
and eat the fruit of them; Take wives, and
beget sons and daughters; and take wives
for your sons, and give your daughters to
husbands, that they may bear sons and
daughters; that you may be increased there,
and not diminished. And seek the peace
of the city into which I have caused you to
be carried away captives, and pray to the
Lord for it: for in its peace shall you have
peace ... For thus says the Lord, that after

seventy years be accomplished at Babylon I
will visit you, and perform my good word
toward you, in causing you to return to
this place."[9]

Jeremiah, the national-spiritual voice of exiled Israel,
offered a different reflection on history and the nature
of exile, urging the Jews to accept their fate as punishment for their sins of idolatry, immoral behaviour and
lack of faith. From the depths of the exile, Jeremiah
urges the Jews to settle down, build new lives and
look to the future.

These two reflections on the journey into exile
represent interesting contrasts, not least because the
exile experience would soon be over and so the journey
home could commence. On reflection, exile produced
a re-working of a previous journey, since having
been redeemed from slavery once in the direction of
Israel, the process would be repeated, this time from
Babylon. The difference was that this time there were
firmer memories of the land, including of the Temple
in Jerusalem, Israelite culture was far more developed

and the journey back was much swifter than 40 years. In 538 BCE, following the edict of Cyrus of Persia, the Jews were permitted to return to their land and rebuild the temple.

Once they returned, a redeemed people could rebuild the Temple and the pilgrimage journey could recommence. Again the surrounding hills would become thick with pilgrims bringing their first fruits and offerings, going upwards to the hills of Jerusalem and beholding the magnificent rebuilt Temple structure. There on the steps of the Temple itself, they would sing one of the inspiring songs of Jewish journeying, later known as a psalm:

> **Psalm 126 A Psalm of Pilgrims**
> *When the Lord brought back the captives to Zion*
> *   we felt like dreamers.*
> *Then our mouths were filled with laughter,*
> *   and our tongues with song.*
> *Even among the nations they said:*
> *   "What great things the Lord has done for them!"*
> *Indeed the Lord has done great things with us!*

How we rejoiced!
Lord, bring back those who cannot return,
like streams in a dry land;
that those who sow in tears
may reap in joy.
Though a man goes out weeping
carrying seed to sow;
he shall come back singing
carrying his sheaves.[10]

The power of the verse is contained in the second line, attempting as it does to express the inner nature of religious experience. Having travelled to Jerusalem bringing the best of their harvests, these farming Jews of the Land of Israel were seeking to reach their God, their source of meaning and salvation.

As a cultural pointer to the significance of the journey, Psalm 126 has particular significance, having been used as the opening section of the Grace after meals service on Sabbaths and festivals. At these special times, the pilgrimage journey is recalled in both a past and future sense. Scattered around the far corners of the exile, one imagines the power of the song to provide a sweet reminder of God's care in past times at the same time as reassuring that there will again be a journey home. 'We were like dreamers' easily slips into being 'we are like dreamers', albeit in changed circumstances.

This joyful journey of return was interrupted with the next cycle of history. Babylon it turned out was only the first of the exiles; the confrontation with the Roman Empire proving to have a far greater impact on the Jewish journey. Situated at the heart of modern-day Rome are the reminders of the former ancient capital of the empire, including the Arch of Titus complete with its iconic frieze depicting the Jews being carried into exile with the holy artifacts of the temple. Built in the year CE 81, to celebrate another victory for the empire, the arch is a dramatic illustration of the next stage in the great Jewish journey. Defeated, humiliated and bruised by their own civil war as well as the power of pagan Rome they found themselves exiled a second time. Less than a mile away on the banks on the River Tiber, captured

Jewish fighters together with the last nominal king of Judea were brought off slave ships to be paraded through the streets. Some were set to work building the Coliseum and other building projects. Fifty years later they were joined by another wave of Jewish captives after the failed uprising led by Bar Kochba, putting an end to all hopes of a sudden restoration to power. This time there would be no Cyrus, no rebuilding and no return; only a long period of readjusting to the complicated ways of the world.

One can only speculate what was going through the minds of those Jews who found themselves on the ships leaving Roman Palestine. Did they know that this journey would define the character of Jewish life for the next 1,900 years? Did they have any conception that the notion of 'home' was changing forever and cultural readjustment, by no means new to Jewish experience, was soon to become a permanent feature of life?

The narrative of exile and return took on new and dramatic form in the nineteenth century in the form of modern Zionism, a movement to kick-start the Jewish journey back to its ancestral homeland. In 1898, the German newspaper *Die Welt* published news of a competition to find a national anthem for the dreamt-of Jewish state. A year earlier, delegates had met in the hall of the Stadtcasino in Basle, Switzerland to found the Zionist movement and set in motion the project for restoring Jewish settlement in the land of Israel. In the terms of secular nationalism, the congress dreamed of ending the Jewish exile and launching the grand Jewish journey home. The anthem was merely a natural addition to that project. The *Die Welt* advertisement did not result in a successful candidate and the search continued to the Fourth Zionist Congress in 1900 where two main contenders were presented. The first was the poem that would eventually be chosen, albeit in adapted form, penned by Naphtali Herz Imber, entitled 'Tikvateinu'. Bursting with historical symbolism, the other contender was Psalm 126.

Imber's winning formulation was eventually adapted to the point where it reads as follows,

As long as the Jewish spirit is yearning deep in
    the heart,
With eyes turned toward the East, looking
    toward Zion,
Then our hope – the two-thousand-year-old hope
    – will not be lost:
To be a free people in our land,
The land of Zion and Jerusalem.

With an appropriately dramatic nationalist flourish
it declares that the Jewish heart always looks towards
the east, to Zion and Jerusalem. Whether or not this
could be proved empirically, or whether the two-
thousand-year hope was never lost, it was undoubt-
edly a powerful testament to the fact that there were
some who still recognized the dispersion as an incom-
plete journey.

Journeys to Jerusalem

With exile came an accepted reality and new types
of journeys came to the fore, beginning with a
reworked version of the pilgrimage of old. Despite

Roman destruction, a significant number of Jews remained in the Land of Israel, who together with others from the diaspora, continued to perform some sort of pilgrimage ritual. Upon arrival at the site in Jerusalem, 'pilgrims' would tear their clothes, one of the outwards signs of a person in mourning. Similarly, others refrained from eating meat or drinking alcohol. The words to be recited were changed, omitting 'A wandering Aramean was my father …' and replacing it with the verse from the book of Isaiah, 'Our holy and beautiful house where our fathers praised You, is burnt with fire and all our pleasant things are laid waste' (Isaiah 64:10). This was a strange new type of journey, almost an 'anti-pilgrimage' designed on the one hand to remember former times and on the other to reinforce the sense of exile.

In later medieval times, a small yet significant number of recorded journeys were also undertaken to the sites of the Holy Land. These were not mass journeys but individual efforts that reconfirmed the centrality of Israel and Jerusalem in Jewish consciousness. Consider the statement by R. Meshullam of

110

Volterra in 1481 who recorded the following,

> On Wednesday 29th July we reached the
> Holy City of Jerusalem and when I saw its
> ruins, I rent my garments a hand breadth,
> and in the bitterness of my heart recited
> the appropriate prayer which I had in a
> small book.[11]

New customs emerged to express the same sentiment.
Rabbi Joseph Karo, who moved to Israel from Turkey
in 1563 records the following in his monumental
and authoritative code of Jewish Law, the *Shulchan
Aruch*.

> A bridegroom puts ashes on his head where
> *tefillin* are worn, in order to remember
> Jerusalem. There are places where the
> custom is to break a glass at the time of the
> wedding ceremony or to place a black cloth
> or other sign of mourning on the head of
> the groom.[12]

The numbers undertaking this journey varied over time. One fifth-century record described 100,000 pilgrims coming, although this seems highly exaggerated. Those who did come tended to come from the near and Middle East, Byzantium, Damascus, Babylon and Egypt. Roughly 1,000 years later, the numbers increased with the influx of Jews from Spain reaching Turkey and the Balkans.

The Wandering Jew: Medieval Jewish Journeys

An irony of the Jewish journey tradition is that the very image of the travelling Jew became a central feature in Christian anti-Jewish iconography. In essence this was just another expression of Christianity's notion of the Jews as the doomed sinners, destined to live their lives as poor wanderers because of their consistent and blind rejection of Jesus as the redeemer. The wandering Jew appears in a popular seventeenth-century legend, published in Germany, that tells of a Jewish shoemaker in Jerusalem taunting Jesus carrying the cross on his way to Calvary, then chasing him away as he attempted to rest on the shoemaker's doorstep. According to the legend Jesus is said to have replied, 'I go but you will roam the earth until I come again.' This is a loose reworking of a phrase used by Jesus in the Gospel of Matthew 'Verily I say unto you, there be some standing here which shall not taste death till they see the Son of Man coming in his kingdom' (16:28), meaning that the Jews will be left wandering until they acknowledge the truth of their folly, at the time of the true redemption. With 40 editions of the legend published in Germany alone before the end of the eighteenth century plus countless others in Dutch, Flemish, French, Spanish and English, the chances are that this was a re-working of an older stereotype of the wandering Jew.

In actual fact the legend was little more than a cultural/theological distortion of an historical reality. The Jews were certainly wanderers in medieval times and even saw themselves as destined to find no permanent resting-place until the final Redemption. Their wandering was part of a self-defined punishment for the breakdown of mutual respect and lack of faith in God, a somewhat different idea of sin from the one claimed by Christianity. In the emerging liturgy of Judaism a key phrase appeared stating *'mipnei chataeinu galinu m'artzeinu'* ('because of our sins we were exiled from our land ...') establishing a very clear self-definition as rootless and suffering. Rootless, however, was one thing, endless wandering was another. The power of the phrase lay in its ability to explain any of the numerous expulsions and forced journeys of history. Through all the catastrophes of medieval Europe; the Crusades (1096); reactions against the Black Death (1348); Spanish Christianity's uprisings against Jews (1391) and so on, the position of the Jews as a vulnerable minority exposed amongst the nations of the world could be explained according to this formula.

Such a dramatic prism for viewing Jewish journeys in the Middle Ages is not sufficient for appreciating what actually happened since other factors were also at work. The journeys of the medieval Jewish world were defined by the twin factors of 'push' and 'pull'. The classic 'push' resulted from the general state of insecurity that hung over all Jewish communities, rendering them vulnerable to periodic expulsion. This resulted in the need to maintain connections with other communities, maintaining awareness of where the next safe haven may need to be found. At the same time, the 'pull' factor reflected the optimistic position of being drawn to places for positive reasons. Invariably this meant finding a local ruler who recognized the benefits of having Jews in their kingdoms, thereby signalling the chance for a new journey. The clergy could rail against the Jew as Christ-killers, but the monarchy saw in the Jews the benefits of loyalty, trade and high taxation.

The numerous negative images of Jews notwithstanding, the folk literature of Europe also offers a different image of the wandering Jew. In Poland for example, where European Jews drifted through the thirteenth century, fascinating images of this phenomenon can be found. One, the legend of Abraham Prochownik, speaks of the arrival of a Jew at a crucial time in Polish history when the nobility were unable to find a new king. Frustrated, they decide that whoever first enters through the city gates the following morning will be regarded as the choice of God. This turns out to be one Abraham Prochownik, a gunpowder merchant who is subsequently declared King of Poland. He declines the offer and is forced to find a clever way to transfer the title to someone else since he does not seek such a position. In this story, the wandering Jew is a merchant on the one hand, but also a wise and an acceptable figure on the other.

In a different and more widely-known legend, the wandering Jew finds Poland as the antidote to wandering. There are numerous versions of this story, including three renditions by Nobel Prize winning writer, S. Y. Agnon, one by the great Yiddish writer I. L. Peretz and others. All are variants of an oral folk tale that present Poland as type of promised land for Jews.

> If you want to know how it suddenly
> occurred to these Jews in Germany to seek
> refuge in Poland, legend has it that after
> the Jews had decreed a fast and beseeched

God to save them from the murderers, a
slip of paper fell from heaven. On it was
written: 'Go to Poland, for there you will
find rest …' The Jews set out for Poland.
When they reached it, the birds in the
forest chirped to greet them: *'Po lin! Po
lin'*. The travellers translated this into
Hebrew, as if the birds were saying: Here
you should lodge …' Afterwards, when
they looked closely at the trees, it seemed
to them that a leaf from the *Gemara* was
hanging on every branch. At once they
understood that here a place had been
revealed to them, where they could settle
and continue to develop the Jewish spirit
and the age-old Jewish learning.[13]

The key to the legend lies in the translation of the term
Poland, *'Po-lin'* or *'Polanya'*, meaning 'rest here' or
'here God rested'. It is a remarkable legend, whereby
Poland takes on the status of a predestined God-
given shelter from the ravages of exile. What is truly

fascinating is the idea of the slip of paper composed in heaven, a sort of divine messaging service, which combines with pages of the Talmud as part of nature, appearing on trees in the forest. In this version, the Jews do not look beyond Poland whereas in others their settlement there is not regarded as permanent since the dream of the return to the Land of Israel is also recognized.

Expulsion

Christian prejudice notwithstanding, it is not inaccurate to see the medieval Jewish journey as one heavily influenced by displacement. Rarely popular with anyone other than the king, the Jews were vulnerable to the whims of political game-playing. The standard aspiration of Jewish communities in Europe was to offer loyalty and service to the king in return for a quiet life with adequate protection and the right to live autonomously within their community institutions. In theory this arrangement could work fine. The problems occurred when other factors came to the fore, ranging from excessive financial pressures to popular anti-Jewish sentiment from religious or mercantile circles. In such situations it was not uncommon for Jews to find themselves unceremoniously expelled, obliged to take up the wanderer's staff again. Take for example the Jews of England, who had crossed the English Channel with William the Conqueror from Normandy in 1066. For just over 100 years, these new Anglo-Jews built good lives for themselves located at strategic places in the medieval English economy. Yet from the late twelfth century onwards their fortunes waned as they faced a rise in religious persecution and more importantly an unsustainable tax burden. Despite some attempts to recast the terms of their employment in the mid-thirteenth century, they were again exploited by a short-sighted fiscal policy. Their inability to pay only proved the point that they had outlived their usefulness and in 1290 they were ordered to leave. The Anglo-Jewish journey had extended Ashkenaz to the far western end of the continent and branched out to many parts of the English countryside. And then it ended sending the Jews back onto their ships across the Channel.

To some degree, the significance of this type of journey stood in direct proportion to the greatness of achievement enjoyed by the community in better times, for example, the Sephardi Jews of the Iberian Peninsula. From the early eighth century, Spain was ruled by the forces of Islam, bringing to the country the culture and wisdom of the Levant. Less fearful of Jews and their beliefs, early Spanish Islamic society offered the possibility for a cultural interchange with another text-based culture. Jews reached high places in the administrations and in some cases even travelled as emissaries for the Muslim rulers. The tenth-century rabbi Hasdai Ibn Shaprut, for instance, became a powerful figure in the Ommayad court in Cordoba where he conducted various diplomatic initiatives for the Caliph. In the next 500 years, Jews experienced a cultural renaissance bequeathing an especially rich legacy in the fields of Hebrew poetry and Jewish philosophy. Thus, when Christianity gathered its forces to re-conquer the land and eventually expelled the entire community, this was more than just another 'moving on'. The departure had in fact begun 100 years earlier when in 1391 the community was attacked by Christian mobs across the country, who killed thousands, causing many others to convert and others to flee. Reflecting on this new departure, one survivor, the poet Solomon de Piera wrote to his friend Moses Gabbai, a Majorcan scholar congratulating him on his decision to quit Spain for North Africa. His words sum up the bitterness of those who had seen the Spanish Jewish dream turn sour.

> *Like to Sodom think thou the Land of Eden,*
> *The home of men that are but verminous things.*
> *Let every sight seem briar and thorn to thee*
> *Change every name, say dogs instead of men.*
> *Rejoicing in the tears of thy tormented ones,*
> *Upon the day of downfall and decay,*
> *They slaughtered thy assailants, broke into*
> *Thy homes, took every stick and stone away.*
> *O may their perfumed incense now emit*
> *A loathsome stench befouling it, and all*
> *Their bread be adder like, their wine turn sour,*
> *Their honey change to wormwood and to gall.*

121

Abhor their food as on Passover,
Think their paradise a very Hell,
And choose the Arab zone to be thine own,
Whether there it shall go ill or well,
And thou shalt wear rich robes or rags. O,
  brother,
Rejoice, for heaven guideth thee. Shun servitude,
Not poverty. Let carobs and coarse bread
Suffice thee, and throw to dogs all richer food.[14]

In the summer of 1492, the great community of Spain departed and yet another Jewish diaspora was created as pre-existing communities were transformed by the arrival of Spanish Jews: in Italy, the Ottoman Empire, the Maghreb, Western Europe and even the Land of Israel.

There was one further journey of expulsion that expresses the drama of the medieval Jewish experience, worth almost nothing in terms of physical distance but everything in terms of symbolism. In 1555, Pope Paul IV issued a Papal Bull taking its name, *'Cum Nimis Absurdum.'* The opening lines translate as, 'Since it is absurd and utterly inconvenient that the Jews, who through their own fault were condemned by God to eternal slavery ...' Demanding that all of Rome's Jews be forced into a ghetto, this was the beginning of a journey that soon swallowed up all the communities of Italy and the Papal States. In the most dramatic and humiliating way possible, it totally defined Jews in relation to place, in a separate and special zone apart from 'civilisation'.

Of the numerous commentaries on this journey of expulsion, a most powerful one can be found in the poem by Crescenzo del Monte (1868–1935) who was born in the Rome ghetto just two years before it was abolished. Written in the unique dialect of the Roman Jews, Judeo Romanesque, the poem provides a dramatic commentary on the relationship between Jews, places and identity.

A Roman Roman

I'm a Roman Jew and I've been Roman
Since the time of "the time of the ancients"
When they were eating their figs

And no one yet spoke Monticiano*

I speak as they spoke then. The strange thing is
That people mock me as if to say:
Look at them – what kind of ancient Romans are you,
Hook noses, going about with your rags and bones?

I've seen Julius Caesar and Pompey.
I've been in trouble with Vespasian,
and it was then that I began to cry Aio-oh**

But with these Aio-oh's I've been able to see
Many houses crumbling step by step,
While I, thank God, am still on my feet.[15]
* Romanesque dialect
**Roman insult meaning something worn
and ragged that would only be sold to a
Jew

Between Two Worlds: Modern Journeys of Leaving and Displacement

An original copy of the early twentieth-century film

'Life of the Jews of Palestine 1913' was recently found in a French film archive. It was an especially remarkable discovery since this unique glimpse of early life in the country was thought to have been lost forever. The film had received its premiere in Europe just before the First World War, after which it disappeared without trace until the late 1990s when by chance a French archive yielded the original nitrate negative. Shot that year on location between Odessa in Southern Russia and the Land of Israel, this was a propaganda film for the early Zionist movement designed to showcase the life of Jews in Palestine at that early stage of development. Its significance for understanding the Jewish journey lies in the poignant and touching opening minutes of the film as it captures the image of groups of bundled-up figures boarding a ship in Odessa. The soon-to-be pioneers are seen waving goodbye to the small crowd of well-wishers below. The gangplank is pulled away and the film captures the moment of departure. Handkerchiefs are waved, tears are wiped, people linger on the quay as others stand by the ship's railings seeing their old home gradually slipping into

125

the past tense. One wonders what was going through their minds? What were they leaving? Why were they leaving? What were they taking with them to their new destination; a place they knew little about? In fact, of equal significance is the question, why they were going to Palestine in the first place? What made them different from the vast majority of Jewish emigrants of that time who sought their fortunes in the New World of the 'goldene medina' – America? The film's distributor in Europe, Yaacov Davidson, commented that when the film was shown in villages and market towns in Europe, 'tears of happiness gleamed in the eyes of Jewish audiences, thirsty for redemption'. Whilst one can understand his interpretation of the weeping, it may just be that the audiences were simply weeping at the scenes of departure since there was hardly a family or community that was not in some way affected by the mass migrations of that time.

In the last 200 years the Jewish world has experienced momentous change. The result of which is a significantly altered map of the Jewish world. It began with the emancipation of the Jews in Western and Central Europe, followed by way of contrast by the massive emigration of non-emancipated Jews from the Russian Empire to North America and other countries of the west. Then the Holocaust reduced the world's Jewish population by one-third, sending most of its survivors looking for new lives far away from their native countries in Europe. At the same time, there has been the general drawing together of scores of communities in the old/new centre in Israel, at the crossing point between Europe, Asia and Africa. The Jewish journey albeit in altered form, has continued to be a defining experience of Jewish life.

Ideological Possibilities

The Russian Jewish writer and activist, Solomon Ansky subtitled his famous drama, 'The Dybuk' as 'Between Two Worlds'. In so doing he bequeathed to modern Jewish culture a description of its defining essence. In almost every way possible, modern Jews have been caught in a bi-polar clamp, Jewish and Gentile, particularist and universalist, inward and outward looking, all the time asking how one moves between them. In Ansky's play the two worlds were those of the rich and poor, the sacred and profane, life and death and finally the seen world and the hidden mystical worlds of Kabbalah. It is a rich and multi-layered work highlighting Ansky's own complex life as he journeyed back and forth across the continent at the crossroads of modernity.

In fact, in one short life Ansky appeared to move everywhere, starting with a journey from the traditional life of a Yeshiva student in Vitebsk to that of a Russian Populist dedicated to the cause of the Russian miners in the Donets Basin. In the style of so many modern Jews, this journey of identity politics led to his adoption of the Russified name, Semyon Akimovich. Yet in the image of the wandering Jew, Ansky did not stay long. Within three years, his health broken, he set out on the road again, this time in the guise of intellectual activist, ending up in St. Petersburg. From there it was to Paris, to the centre of the European revolutionary world, now as a member of the Socialist Revolutionary Party. By the early years of the twentieth century, Ansky was able to identify as a Jew again, albeit a radical one, finding affinity with the revolutionary outlook of the Bund (General Jewish Workers Union of Poland, Lithuania and Russia), leaving his permanent mark in the form of their anthem 'Die Shvue' ('The Oath'). Then in 1905, following vicious anti-Jewish pogroms across the Pale of Settlement and the outbreak of the first Russian revolution, he began a clearer journey back to the affairs of his People. He spent time with Zionist activists in Geneva before returning to St. Petersburg and a final shift to the world of ethnography, documenting and celebrating the folk culture of the Jews. By the end of his life in November 1920, he had moved to Vilna and then to Warsaw. By then he had conducted two lengthy and significant journeys into the heartland of the Galician *shtetl*, at first to collect evidence and artifacts of Jewish life and then to document the destructive effects of the First World War.

Ansky's life was a constant journey between worlds, between heart and mind, always seeking new answers and for this reason he is a fitting emblem for the period. There were others however, thousands if not millions of them, whose lives, even if not as dramatic were no less caught up in the same process. What Ansky and so many others sought was a truthful reflection of their inner spirit enabling them to live successfully in the new world around them. For many this was, in the best traditions of Jewish journeys, both a physical and a spiritual journey.

Journeys Out of the Ghetto

Throughout the nineteenth and twentieth centuries, Jews changed address, making that crucial journey from the streets they had known for centuries to new areas further afield. At first this meant travelling a relatively short distance away from the Jewish quarter and into the rest of the city but emotionally, psychologically and culturally this was a distance far greater than the physical distance would suggest. This was a journey to another world.

Consider the example of the Jews of Budapest, who journeyed around the environs of their city for over 1,000 years only to end up a few kilometres from where they started. Contemporary visitors to Budapest cannot fail to miss the stunning Moorish-styled minarets atop the cathedral-like synagogue on Dohany Street at the heart of modern Pest. This remarkable structure is the second-largest synagogue in the world, the biggest in Europe and boasts one of the largest set of organ pipes in Hungary. As such it is a first rate symbol of the Jewish journey of modernity, a massive monument to emancipation, advancement and change. Built in 1859, the Dohany synagogue pre-dates full Jewish citizenship in Austro-Hungary by eight years and was thus designed to speak as much of aspirations as achievements. During the service of dedication, the address was delivered by Chief Rabbi Alois Wolf Meisel who made a point of thanking God for the new building as well as the Hungarian homeland and the Emperor. One could have been mistaken for thinking that the Jews had always been happy, contented residents of this city even though the story was far more complicated. In fact, the synagogue was built by Jews who until a decade earlier had been unable to reside permanently in the city, living instead on a temporary basis in the 'Orczy Houses', a crowded and cramped set of structures nearby. Furthermore, even the Orczy Houses were a mid-nineteenth century concession. The journey into Budapest was not straightforward.

Jews had lived on the Buda side of the River Danube since medieval times, and from the thirteenth century close to the castle on Jew's Street. Following their expulsion for not converting to Christianity in 1360, they returned to find their homes taken and were obliged to move to the edge of the city, in Tanhacs Mihaly street. There they remained for 3,000 years including during the period of Turkish rule when, freed from the strictures of Christianity, their lives temporarily improved. In 1686 they were slaughtered in great numbers by the invading Austrians and the survivors banished from the city. It took the generosity of a liberally-minded noblemen, Count Zilchy in nearby Obuda, to save the Jews from having to leave the area altogether. Remarkably, in 1848, the Jews of Obuda proudly stood outside their synagogue in Obuda and handed over the adornments from their

'Sifrei Torah' (scrolls of the Law) to the nationalist rebels of the Hungarian uprising, determined to show that as modernity beckoned, they wished to throw in their lot with their Magyar neighbours. The revolution failed and it would take a sojourn in the Orczy Houses and two more decades before Jews could find their place at the heart of city. Despite a presence predating the Magyars themselves, the journey to the heart of civic life took over 1,000 years.

Having arrived, the Jews quickly prospered and soon comprised the majority of the city's professional middle class. Yet on a social level it was clear that the journey was far from over. Prejudice lingered and there remained zones of exclusion. It seemed that the bourgeois city of Budapest was not shy of allowing prejudice and social rejection of Jews to be a norm. Writing at the start of the twentieth century, the liberal aristocrat, Count Miklos Zay acknowledged this,

> In 1897, I was the president of the great
> evening ball in the capital. When the

time came to issue invitations, I was
embarrassed to hear that Jewish families
did not at all appear on the roster. For a
while, I protested, but the members of
the organising committee insisted that if
Jews were to be invited, those who usually
attend the ball will keep away. Personally
I became convinced of the truth of this
allegation.[16]

However, there were other far more significant
holdups on the journey. In 1868, the Hungarian
Parliament sought Jewish representatives for its
Upper House, since religious groups were entitled
to a place in the legislature. Yet the full drama of
the journey into modernity came to the fore when
the Jewish 'community' met to choose their representatives since no agreement could be reached.
Along the way, divergent paths had been taken by
those attempting to balance their commitment to
being Jewish alongside that of being a modern and
rational member of European culture. The new

movement known as *'Neolog'* in Hungary ('Reform', 'Conservative' elsewhere) initiated liturgical, ritual and in some cases theological changes. The service contained sections in the local language and an organ was used to beautify the service, all of which was unacceptable to the Orthodox traditionalists. With no agreement on matters of Jewish identity and culture there could be no agreement on representation before the Hungarian parliament. The only reasonable path was to part company and have the state recognize two distinct and separate Jewish communities. In two generations, the journey into the modern world brought the Jews into the heart of the city where they promptly parted company.

Elsewhere in Europe the story was played out in similar terms, only varying according to the nuanced conditions of each place. In Prague, the third city of the Austro-Hungarian Empire, a 'commentator' came to the fore whose very art seemed to reflect the dilemma of living both in the two domains of the Jewish community and the new and changing world around. Franz Kafka was born in a house whose entrance opened out into the streets of the former Jewish quarter, a separate Jewish town that had housed the closed community for centuries. However, the windows of the house looked out to the edges of the Old Town Square in Gentile Prague, where Jews had recently been permitted to live. Kafka wrote in German, one of the last Jews to write in the language of the empire as opposed to Czech, the language of the rising national movement.

Finally, even in otherwise-liberal Prague anti-Semitism reared its ugly head to remind all, including Kafka, that one never fully arrived in the modern world as a Jew without prejudice and one remained in a strange space between old and new. In one of his numerous letters to his 'lover', Milena Jesenska, he writes,

> Every afternoon I now walk along the
> streets and bathe in anti-Semitism.
> 'Prasive plemono' [filthy race] I have now
> once heard the Jews referred to. Is it not
> absolutely obvious that you leave behind

the place where you are hated ... The
heroism that consists in staying anyway is
that of the cockroaches which cannot even
be exterminated from the bathroom.

I have just looked out of the window:
mounted police, gendarmerie with their
bayonets ready to attack, the screaming
masses running in all directions, and up
here at the window the revolting disgrace
of having to live the whole time in
refuge.[17]

Modernity offered the Jews a chance to reverse the
journeys of the ghetto, to travel only a short distance
into new suburbs and streets but at the same time
intellectually, spiritually and culturally to cross
centuries. Some of the time it worked and at others it
was no more than an illusion.

Emigration and the Great 'Churban'
For all his travels, physical and ideological, Ansky
and others like him remained within the European

domain, predominantly the East. Being between the worlds of the *yeshiva* in Vitebsk and the mines of Donets there was still continuity, of ruler, of Jewish society and of broader cultural milieu.

By far the dominant journeys of the modern period were those undertaken by emigrants departing the lands of Eastern Europe for the West. In a 50-year period, between the last quarter of the nineteenth century and the first quarter of the twentieth, close to three million Jews from the Russian Empire and surrounding areas joined the great trek to America, Britain, Canada, and beyond. Certainly this journey can be placed in the context of previous relocations discussed earlier. There were certainly similar push and pull factors; the effects of economic dislocation and political violence offset against the lure of the developing societies of North America and the openness of Britain. Yet there were also distinct differences since these new lands were far advanced in the journey to modernity.

The journey of the emigrant was by no means straightforward: decisions had to be made and pitfalls avoided. For instance, whilst many left as family units, it was perfectly normal for the young male to go ahead and establish himself before bringing over his wife, children, parents or all of them. It was not unheard-of for the young male to 'lose his way', consciously or unconsciously, abandoning all he had left behind. Then there were single women who travelled alone, only to be preyed upon at the docks by white slavers and sold into prostitution. Similarly there were Christian missionaries, unscrupulous ticket agents, slum landlords and exploitative employers. Yet, inevitably, the experience of the emigrant went far beyond the process of leaving and arriving.

Whether pushed or pulled, there was another plain but crucial fact of life for the emigrant, namely that the journey ensured a rapid encounter with modernity in all its forms. Confronted by the thrilling experience of living as citizens in countries that respected the rule of law, promoted principles of liberty and justice and encouraged initiative, it was hard for the journey to cease when the ship docked. Furthermore, once the movement began, completely new networks of Jewish living came to the fore to mediate the transition. These were in the form of self-help organizations, '*landsman-schaft*' (organization of former residents of the same city or village). The effect of these networks cannot be underestimated since they softened the landing of the new immigrants. The Jewish quarters of the new East European diaspora in New York, London, Montreal and elsewhere were filled with institutions that read like the map of Poland or Lithuania. These *landsmanschaft* were an interesting commentary on the Jewish relationship with 'place'. No-one was under any illusion that the immigrant Jew felt an affinity with Russia, Poland or Lithuania as countries, but with Narevker, Mogilevoner or Kalish there was a fully-fledged love affair. Distance did nothing but intensify the sense of connectedness.

Inevitably, emigration meant that acculturation was a given for the next generation of Jews. To a greater or lesser degree, and within one generation, emigrants had become immigrants, and acquired a hyphen in their identity, being no longer just Jews but now American-Jews, British-Jews and Canadian-Jews. Everything was up for grabs, whole areas of

Jewish life were challenged and changed: Yiddish went from being a mother tongue to be the tongue of one's mother, a secondary language after English; clothes changed as head coverings were hidden or disappeared; ritual fringes were tucked in or taken off; religious practices in general were modified to fit the demands of a secular society and eventually economic advancement and physical security changed the very self image of the Jews themselves.

The journey across continents and from one reality to another had the potential to leave a trail of cultural dislocation in its wake. There were many who naturally lapped up the opportunity to leave the old world behind, adapt to the new milieu with Jewishness gradually slipping to a secondary level of identity. Yet there were others who, whilst welcoming the clear benefits of safety, freedom and economic advancement always knew that a price would be paid culturally. Some came to see the departure from Eastern Europe as a type of '*Churban*' ('destruction'), the Hebrew term used to describe the destruction of the Temples in Jerusalem. Whatever the reasons for leaving there was no getting away from the fact that the Yiddish language steadily declined after departure as did the intensity of learning and general Jewish life.

End of the Journey

The journey into the modern world claimed many casualties on the way – physically, spiritually and emotionally. Demographically, thousands, if not millions of Jews managed to disappear from view without fanfare or loud declaration but simply by following the path from acculturation to assimilation. Across a few generations, residence gradually changed from the Jewish quarter, *shtetl* or area to the new streets, suburbs and cities where other Jews simply did not live. Culturally, it happened by following the simple logic of accepting the society around on its own terms, speaking its language, attending its schools, learning its history, memorizing its poets and imbibing its values. Physically, the notion of 'casualties' is considerably more raw since it is only in the modern world, and in the terms of the modern world with its technologies, systems of thought and changed moral order that mass murder took Jews on their final Jewish journey.

There were no shortage of commentators to reflect on the drama as it was unfolding. One was the Yiddish writer, Jacob (Yankev) Glatstein whose own life came close to all the dramas described so far. Born in Lublin in 1896, he emigrated to the United States at the age of eighteen in 1914 where he enrolled at law school only to give it up a year later and become a teacher and writer. Glatstein was a key mover in a literary group known as the '*Inzikhistn*', meaning 'in the self' or 'introspectivists', who wished to assert a purely aesthetic approach to writing, divorcing it from politics or ideology. The idea, whilst managing to keep its modernist form, did not separate itself from engaging with the larger issues of the Jewish drama. Critically, in 1934 Glatstein travelled back to Europe to Poland via Germany. In both countries he came face to face with the rising tide of anti-Jewish hatred and violence leading him to muse upon its significance. On a literary level, the personal confrontation produced two pieces, a novel and a poem, both of which are highly significant as reflections on the Jewish journey. In the first, 'Ven Yash iz Geforn' ('When Yash Goes Forth'), the narrator is Glatstein himself who reverses the direction of the conventional journey, instead of leaving Europe he arrives in it. The former emigrant now makes a journey of return even though to all intents and purposes he feels an outsider. He is the success story of modernity. Yet the crisis he encounters however gives rise to a second piece, blistering in its anger and rejection of modernity.

Goodnight, World

Goodnight, wide world,
Great, stinking world.
Not you, but I slam the gate.
With the long gabardine,
with the yellow patch – burning –
with proud stride
I decide -:
I am going back to the ghetto.
Wipe out, stamp out all traces of apostasy.
I wallow in your filth.

Blessed, blessed, blessed,
hunchbacked Jewish life.
Go to hell, with your polluted cultures, world.
Though all is ravaged,
I am dust of your dust,
sad Jewish life.

Prussian pig and hate filled Pole;
Jew killers, land of guzzle and gorge.
Flabby democracies, with your cold
sympathy compresses.
Goodnight, electro-impudent world.
Back to my kerosene, tallowed shadows,
eternal Octobers, minute stars,
to my warped streets and hunchbacked lanterns,
my worn-out pages of the Prophets,
my Gemaras, to arduous
Talmudic debates, to lucent, exegetic Yiddish,
To Rabbinical Law, to deep deep meaning, to
   duty, to what is right.
World, I walk with joy to the quiet ghetto light.

Good night. It's all yours, world. I disown
my liberation.
Take back your Jesusmarxists, choke on their
  arrogance.
Croak on a drop of our baptized blood.
And though He tarries, I have hope;
day in, day out, my expectation grows.
Leaves will yet green
on our withered tree.
I don't need any solace.
I return to our cramped space.
From Wagner's pagan music to chants of sacred
  humming.
I kiss you, tangled strands of Jewish life.
Within me weeps the joy of coming home.[18]

Betrayed, confused and defeated by his journey to the
inner courtyards of modernity, citizenship, ideology
and culture, Glatstein calls for a retreat, a return
journey to the elusive world of 'home'. Written after
the rise of Nazism but crucially before the killing, the
retreat will not bring redemption but simply reduce

the anguish when the greater forces of modernity at their most destructive are finally revealed.

The journeys of the modern world were both spatial and symbolic. The physical locations of traditional Europe with its compact Jewish sociology and intense Jewish culture were exchanged for new lives in new worlds. This journey away turned out to be powerfully subversive, generating whole new genres of Jewish self-expression. The retrospective look through those journeys, however, appears troubling and confusing, with too many images mired with feelings of rejection, failure and destruction. Yet it is also clear that Glatstein's rallying cry of 'Goodnight, world ... within me weeps the joy of coming home' could be no more than a rhetorical flourish since the processes of history could not be reversed. Furthermore, it sidesteps other less bi-polar verdicts on modernity that could still appreciate the advancements made by Jews. What is clear is that the ambiguities and complexities of modernity have given rise to a new chapter in the history of Jewish travel, the contemporary journey for restored meaning and identity.

Modern Journeys of Redemption: Returning to the Land of Israel

By the shores of Lake Kinneret in Israel sits a beautiful cemetery with palm trees and the graves of pioneers from the early collective farms and settlements dating back to a time known as the Second *Aliya* (lit. ascent, meaning immigration to Israel). Inscribed are names of Jews, mostly of Eastern European origin who are identified by dates of birth, death and date of their arrival in the country. At the other end of the country, in the Negev desert by Kibbutz Sde Boker, is the grave of David Ben Gurion, the first Prime Minister of Israel and 'father of the nation'. His grave lists only date of immigration and death, testament to his belief that his life only truly began when he arrived in the homeland. Finally, on the graves of all soldiers buried in military graves the inscription insists on listing the place from where the fallen soldier originated. A consistent message emerges from all these examples, that the rebirth of these Jews, collectively and individually began with the journey to the Land of Israel.

Significantly, the journey did not occur as prophesied in Biblical texts: it was led by primarily secular Jews consciously attempting to remake the Jewish People in a new form. These were the small minority of Jews who did not head west to America at the time of the emigrations, but chose instead the seemingly ludicrous journey to the east, to the Land of Israel. Inspired by the intellectual and ideological shifts in European Jewish Enlightenment, they sought to rebuild and recast the Jewish People into a different state of being, 'a free nation in its homeland'. It was partly a psychological assertion of group pride and self esteem and partly a call for physical transformation, but here were modern-day Abrahams departing their homes in the Diaspora to find better ones in the Land of Israel. In this national project there would be no mention of '*Churban*' ('destruction', as used earlier to describe the loss of Eastern European heritage), to describe the cultural revolution that would occur. Instead a new vocabulary would be nurtured, transforming the traditional religious language of redemption into a secular nationalist guise. And so a modern Israeli cultural canon was born overflowing with journey motifs. The iconic phrases of early-twentieth century Zionist idealism could be found in the following song lyrics.

> I. *Anu banu artzah, livnot u'lehibanot*
> We have come to the Land to build and be
>   built

> II. *Artza alinu ... k'var charashnu v'gam*
>   *zaranu aval od lo katzarnu*
> We have gone up to our land ... we have
>   ploughed and planted but we have not
>   yet harvested our crop.

Sung by pioneers, youth movement members and schoolchildren alike, these were the secular prayers of pioneers redeeming themselves and their land. The redemption would be carried out by strapping young workers, not God. This image can be seen in visual form in such early Zionist cinema such as in Helmar Laski's 1935 film 'Avodah', built upon a powerful journey motif. It opens with the following quotation from the Bible,

> And he shall set up a banner for the nations
> and shall assemble the outcasts of Israel
> and gather together the dispersed of Judah
> from the four corners of the earth.[19]

What follows, however, is far from an expression of classical religious iconography but a thoroughly modern presentation of the New Jew, the symbolic hero of the Zionist revolution. Stylistically, it is heavily influenced by socialist realism presenting the journey of one pioneer and his journey home. Like the film 'Life of the Jews of Palestine 1913' it opens with a departure, but this time with no bundled people waving to weeping relatives on the quay, only an anonymous pair of feet. The feet walk and walk, climbing hills, along roads and railway tracks until eventually the music announces a point of arrival. Only then does the camera steadily rise up the body to reveal the identity of the traveller – a smiling, strapping young man who looks confidently to the left and right, surveying the area before setting off on his new life.

In the Zionist treatment of the Jewish journey, several versions of travel emerge. The first is that of departure/arrival, from *'galut'* ('exile' – Zionism preferred this value-laden term to the neutral 'diaspora') to *'moledet'* ('motherland'). However, like the internal pilgrim in post-settlement Biblical Israel there would be other journeys to be made such as the *'tiyul'* ('hike'). The new Jews of the modern Land of Israel sought to draw closer to the *'moledet'* by working it, walking it, digging it and building it; elevating hiking to an act of profound symbolic value. A normal nation, argued the ideologists, is in touch with its land, its seasons, geography, topography, flora and fauna. So, armed with a Bible and a guide to flowers and plants, the new Jews set off to become one with the land.

Travel books come in all shapes and sizes and the Bible was the ultimate volume for the new Jewish hiker. Of the many national tasks to accomplished, for the individual and the group was to prove and reinforce one's rootedness in the land. What better way than by finding the past in the ground, as a real part of the present. The discovery of Biblical Israel could be read in the written text of the Bible and in the physical text of the land; in the description of Abraham's purchase of the Cave of Machpelah in Hebron; Deborah's victory at Mount Tavor and the numerous references to the Temple in Jerusalem. Never had the Bible been used by Jews for such secular pursuits.

The *tiyul* could be used to connect with specific moments in history with extra resonance, such as Masada. Prior to the destruction of the Temple, a group of Jewish Zealots fled to the former Herodian stronghold of Masada where they holed themselves up in defiance of the Roman expectation of complete surrender. For three years after the destruction they held out against the Romans, believing themselves to be the last free Jewish men and women in the Land of Israel. As the Romans eventually drew close and scaled the mountain, they committed group suicide rather than die at the hands of the enemy.

Such heroic passion spoke directly to the soul of the Zionist pioneers for whom the mountain became a powerful symbol of their own determination to be masters of their own fate. In the days before a proper road through the Judean desert had been completed, the *tiyul* to Masada was a dangerous mission necessitating carrying several days' supply of food and water. Then there was the perilous climb up the mountain itself, before the neat paths or the cable-car of today had been installed. The journey took on an aura of challenge, testing the mettle of those who attempted it and conferring a badge of honour on those who succeeded. There were some who died on this particular Jewish journey. In short, the Masada journey had all the characteristics of the Zionist journey; physical challenge, idealistic symbolism and historical connection. For a time it was even chosen as a fitting location for swearing-in Israeli soldiers in certain units. It is all the more ironic given the eventual questioning of this 'Masada myth' by later generations who question whether the Zealots should be held up as good examples of Jewish behaviour in the first place. Modern-day visitors to Masada tend to arrive in buses in order to see the sunrise and not for ideological inspiration

The only problem with such descriptions of modern Zionist journeys is the assumption that everything indeed worked according to the ideological frame – everything was collective, assured and good. There were many who arrived with a more pragmatic and less ideologically driven approach to the new land, just as there were others whose Zionism was cast in a variant political hue. At some point one cannot help asking if there was any expression of subversion, recognition that collective history making was not the only way of seeing things. In a typically beautiful and honest description the Israeli novelist Amos Oz recounts the following image,

> Often around 5 or 6 o clock I see an elderly
> woman on the kibbutz sitting on a bench
> singing to herself, and I don't know what
> she sings because it's Polish. And I think
> to myself: That woman 45 years ago must

155

have been a romantic girl with braids
sitting by a stream somewhere in Poland
singing in Hebrew about Jerusalem ...[20]

Contemporary Jewish Journeys

The rules of Jewish travel have been re-written in
the contemporary world largely because the terms of
Jewish living have also. On a general level, travel itself
has taken on a new significance becoming a leisure
pursuit, such as playing golf or doing home improve-
ments; all are expressions of 'who we are' and how we
live. Across the class divide, all sections of Western
society have embraced travel as a desirable pursuit,
conveying a sense of value and even status. One may
even say that in terms of identity people are defined
by the travel choices that they make. Jews are part and
parcel of this process, presenting the obvious question
of why Jews make Jewish choices when they travel.

For many (but by no means all), Jewish travel has
come to serve a radically new function in life, becoming
one element in the journey of constructing and com-
pleting Jewish identity. Given the multi-dimensional

nature of identity in the contemporary world, Jewish travel will never represent the total expression of a person's inner self since that self has many allegiances and characteristics. The Jewish one, however, has the potential to rise higher than other elements given its potential for deep feelings of authenticity and meaning. Therefore, the idea of journey could not be better for the contemporary Jew in search of a part of life that is connected and purposeful. In fact the very encounter with stories of other Jews in other places and periods offer exciting and inspiring environments in which to discover themselves.

In recent years there appears to be a type of Jewish 'Grand Tour' emerging, offering travel to the Jewish equivalents of the temples and palaces of culture that so attracted the gentlemen and ladies of the eighteenth and nineteenth centuries. Those original Grand Tour travellers sought to broaden their cultural horizons and gain a broader view of their world by visiting the sites of antiquity as well as the new symbols of advancement of the time. The Jewish Grand Tour traveller is also interested in broadening horizons, expanding a sense of who they are in relation to the 'tribe' and maybe seeking a reflection of themselves in the mirror of history.

The two central locations for the Jewish 'Grand Tour' are Israel and Poland, representing a wide range of Jewish expressions of identity. Admittedly there are some who choose to make genealogy the basis of their travels and others choose from the broad range of other Jewish locations including Prague, Budapest, parts of Germany, Andalusian Spain, Morocco and Italy. Yet, repeatedly it is Israel and Poland that stand out as the dominant destinations. What do these sites represent and what do they suggest about the inner world of the contemporary Jewish journey?

For one thing, they point to the emergence of a Jewish identity characterized by ethnicity in general and ethnic pride in particular. In the case of Israel and Poland, these translate easily into distinct types of Jewish travel programme, aided by the ever-developing range of organized programmes for all ages, including those whose names make it quite clear the nature of the trip, such as the previously mentioned 'March of the Living' and 'From Anguish to Hope', which deliberately combine visits to both countries. This new Jewish Grand Tour does not come without a host of complexities and unanswered questions.

Jewish Journeys to Poland

The ambiguous nature of mass Jewish tourism to Poland lies at the heart of the following piece taken from the script of a recent Israeli television satire,

> Travel agent (on the phone): "We have
> a few specials for Poland that I really
> recommend. First of all, we have the basic
> package, which includes five concentration
> camps in 10 days, accommodation in
> four-star hotels in Warsaw and a free day
> for shopping there. Beyond that we, of
> course, have 'Classic Poland' in 14 days,
> including visits to seven concentration
> camps, accommodation in four-star hotels
> and a visit to the Warsaw Ghetto with
> the afternoon free for shopping. We also

have a weekend in Poland, which features
seven concentration camps in three days
– no, there's no free day for shopping. And
naturally there's the 12-day cross-Poland
package with all the concentration camps
… My sister's daughter went on a trip
like that with her school and it was very
impressive. She cried at Auschwitz."[21]

Holocaust, identity and travel all fuse together in this
sharp satire on Polish Jewish tourism. What indeed
does one expect from a visit to a country where one-
third of the Jewish people were murdered? The sites
of Polish Jewish tourism are certainly bizarre since
almost everything seems to have been touched by the
angel of death: forests where hundreds of thousands of
Jews were murdered in cold blood; locations of great
synagogues destroyed by the Nazis; endless cemeteries in towns, cities and villages where many of the
graves have been destroyed; sites of death camps;
memorials and then the occasional museums celebrating the contribution of Jews to Polish life? How on

earth can these be woven into a coherent narrative that expresses the search of contemporary Jews to find something meaningful?

This is especially poignant since there is no precedent for Jews revisiting the sites of their massacres in times past. Previously the main concern would have been to ensure proper burial for the dead and the marking of their graves. Hundreds of visitors from abroad with flags and guitars, a typical picture of organized Jewish tourism to Poland, is quite a different 'performance'. This is a new and strange phenomenon and one not without the potential for distorting the conventions of previous Jewish journeys.

Increasingly, from the 1980s, Jewish groups began visiting Poland in large numbers, propelled by the desire to respond to two powerful sets of emotions. The first was that of Jewish pride inspired by the ongoing story of Jewish survival in the world, despite the destruction so evident in Poland. This fed into a powerful campaign to promote greater and more intense Jewish identity amongst participants by proclaiming that in spite of everything the Nazis did, the

Jewish People lives ('*Am Yisrael Chai*'). The second was that of Jewish roots, seeking out a story of Jewish community and culture in Poland that could in theory offer a deeper sense of self in the more complicated reality of late twentieth century modernity. In a crude way, visiting Poland was a chance for Jews to enter the film set of 'Fiddler on the Roof', to somehow be strengthened by its idyll of secure identity and maybe even experience a little of its adoration of 'tradition'.

In so doing, this new type of Jewish journey took on characteristics of what may called 'secular pilgrimage', the visitation of sacred sites where the individual can be deeply touched, transformed and experience a greater wholeness. Indeed many of the rites of tourism are performed, quite often by people who would otherwise never undertake anything similar elsewhere: ceremonies are held where traditional prayers referring to God are recited along with distinctly secular poems and readings; solemn songs are sung; candles are lit; participants are encouraged to talk about their feelings and open emotional expression is encouraged.

Yet often it is not entirely clear what the message of the trips are: to honour the dead of the Holocaust?; to recall the remarkable cultural diversity of the pre-war community?; to find answers to profound questions of meaning in the face of the extremities of the Holocaust? Or to declare to the world that the Jewish People is strong again and will never be vulnerable as it was 'then'? There are certainly those in Israel who use organized journeys to Poland to reinforce messages of power as a reflection of their own needs to be strong in the face of ongoing war. Bizarrely there are many for whom Poland is considered the best vehicle for promoting Jewish identity and fighting assimilation. With this multiplicity of messages and objectives, the volume of Jewish tourist traffic to Poland continues to grow.

The heritage aspect of Polish Jewish journeys is also challenging with no clear statement of what is being sought. Most contemporary Jews live different Jewish lives to those of pre-war Poland, and whilst intrigued by them do not necessarily want to adopt them. Furthermore, for those wishing to see how

Jews lived, the simple yet painful truth is that the old pre-war community is no more. Yiddish can no longer be heard on the streets of former '*shtetlech*' or Jewish quarters and the existing Jewish community is a wholly different phenomenon to its pre-1939 ancestor. To make this journey remotely feasible the traveller must be prepared to rely on their imagination since the sites are often absent spaces and lost voices. They must be willing to make do, for instance, with reading from the works of Jewish writers at the sites of their destroyed houses and other similarly bizarre performances.

In Poland, most Jewish groups ignore contemporary Poland, preferring to rely instead on negative pre-war stereotypes of anti-Semitic prejudice. Many official Israeli school groups go as far as hiring security guards, theoretically to protect the participants from potential attackers but in the end succeed only in ensuring that the participants never encounter, see or experience a Poland that is not filtered through official channels. Similarly the narrative presented on the trip rarely finds time to acknowledge Poland's own history or let its concerns seep in.

And yet, in spite of all these questions, there remains something consistently powerful about such journeys, representing as they do the need of a later generation to bear witness to what happened and to dedicate themselves to drawing appropriate conclusions. Strange and uncomfortable though it looks to some, there are many who are inspired by the powerful symbolism of seeing Israeli flags in places where Jews were killed in their millions. Similarly, there are many for whom the greatest significance of visiting Poland is simply to draw strength from seeing living Jews discovering more about their people in sites where enemies tried to stamp out Jewish life forever. Ironically, there are many who use the distinctively Jewish experience of a group visit to Poland to seek and declare universal messages, from the need to fight prejudice to the celebration of all forms of cultural diversity.

There are few easy conclusions to draw regarding contemporary Jewish travel to Poland. It is tempting to compare such journeys to magnifying glasses, simply enlarging the opinions and beliefs of those participating, or those organizing them. If one believed in the need for Jewish power, or religious conviction, or universal values or strong Jewish identities, going to Poland only strengthens that conviction.

Jewish Journeys to Israel

In any given summer, recent years of violence notwithstanding, Israel's Ben Gurion airport witnesses a remarkable expression of contemporary Jewish travel. Tens of thousands of Diaspora Jews converge on the country for anything between two and six weeks seeking mixed doses of relaxation and Jewish inspiration, whilst a similar number of Jewish Israeli citizens depart the country in search of doses of relaxation and inspiration away from the intensity of Jewish life at home. All are participating in the drama of contemporary Jewish life.

For the incoming tourist the sites on offer are quite breathtaking. These include 3,000-year-old symbols of Biblical antiquity alongside symbols of modern Israeli sovereignty; innovative expressions of global culture in the language of the Bible alongside performances of Jewish cultural and ethnic diversity – unprecedented in Jewish history. All the journey requires to get going is the answer to one simple question, namely how does the tourist regard all this?

The choices are clear. For some this is simply observer tourism, watching and enjoying something without allowing it to touch one's inner self. For others, this is a tempting array of potential experiences connected with being Jewish, some of which may be inspiring and even transformative. The Bible of weekly Hebrew school could potentially be made to come alive, as could the sense of connectedness with a historical drama and collective memory. And then there are those for whom this would always be a sacred experience, a true expression of who they wish to be, from the religious observant to the secular nationalist.

Along the way, tourists are challenged to relate to both the territorial and the sociological aspects of Israel: the physical drama of the land complete with buildings, battles sites and Biblical dramas on the one hand and the people, lifestyles and values of society on the other. The Western Wall in Jerusalem's Old City has been the focal point of Jewish memory and yearning for almost 2,000 years. Where does it fit on a journey alongside a nightclub stuffed full of twenty-something Hebrew speakers, all of whom are second or third generation immigrants from the Jewish Diaspora?

Unlike traditional Jewish journeys to the Land of Israel, many contemporary ones seek links between Israel and the Diaspora, adopting a rather utilitarian approach to the impact of such journeys. It has been the assumption of funders and officials in the Jewish world that the 'Israel Experience' has the greatest chance of transforming the lives of contemporary Jews, moving them closer to the point when being Jewish is the centre of their identity; hoping that the excitement of being Jewish in Israel will somehow generate bonds of loyalty and purpose. Such is the confidence that newer and better targeted programmes are marketed, including the most recent, the dramatically titled 'Birthright' programme, funded as a joint project of the Israeli government and Diaspora Jewish organizations. In ten short days, a 21-year-old marginally affiliated Jew from Texas, Johannesburg or London can actualize their 'right' to see the Land of Israel and be part of its Jewish community. By the time they return home, less than two weeks after arriving, it is hoped that the physical journey will have sparked an interest that will result in pursuing a more considered and committed Jewish life.

If 'Birthright' is the most recent dramatically-titled journey, 'March of the Living' belongs to the previous wave, the most clearly definable expression of modern secular pilgrimage. Beginning in the death camps of Poland, this programme proceeds to Israel where the participants affirm the power of Jewish survival and make some attempt to enjoy Israeli 'normality', in shopping malls, beaches and meeting 'real Israelis'. 'March' participants return with home enjoined to all the dramas of Jewish history, committed to a Jewish future and continuity.

Statistically, there has never been a situation when

so many Jews in the world have visited Israel. Aside from the fact that just under half of world Jewry live there, recent statistics have shown that some 78 per cent of Anglo-Jews have visited the country, 35 per cent of American Jews and 66 per cent of Canadian Jews. Steadily, as the crowds flow through Ben Gurion airport, the Jewish People is re-acquainting itself with Israel.

Conclusion

Deutscher was mistaken, since Jewish legs are also their roots. It is true there is little that is static about the Jews, especially when it comes to physical space, but legs sometimes tire and need to rest. Legs do not act without instructions and there are other parts of the body telling them to return to where they came from, to move to avoid danger and also to stop and appreciate the place where they are.

Voices and Places:
Literary Jewish Journeys
through the Ages

To return to the question that opened this book, what does one pack for a Jewish journey? More specifically, what literature should be read? By linking words to places, the potential dialogue of the journey is more complex and the experience far richer. In fact, the addition of text allows the traveller the chance to go beyond the *'peshat'* (the rabbinic term for simple interpretation), to the realm of *'derash'* (deeper interpretation or extrapolation). The challenge is in the selection, matching words to places, finding the texts that will tease out the essence of a place, or allow the visitor to see it from a different angle.

Nothing is straightforward in this regard. Descriptive texts, for instance, belong in guidebooks which are certainly not the same. Texts that only praise the site, speaking only of its beauty, can become tiresome since it is rare to find a place with no rough edges. Ultimately, the challenge of putting words to places lies as much with the reader as with the words since what matters is the way one interprets them. Consider for instance a journey to twenty-first century Bialystok, birthplace of Ludwig Zamenhof, creator of the Esperanto language, almost 150 years since his birth.

I was born in Bialystok in the province of
Grodno. This place where I was born and
spent my childhood gave the direction
to all my future endeavours. In Bialystok
the population consisted of four diverse
elements: Russians, Poles, Germans and
Jews: each spoke a different language and
was hostile towards the other elements.
In this town, more than anywhere else,
an impressionable nature feels the heavy
burden of linguistic differences and is
convinced, at every step, that the diversity

of language is the only, or at least the main
cause that separates the human family and
divides it into conflicting groups. I was
brought up as an idealist; I was taught that
all men were brothers, and, meanwhile,
in the street, in the square, everything at
every step made me feel that 'men' did not
exist, only Russians, Poles, Germans, Jews
and so on.[1]

The traveller is obliged to consider the truth of this
contention. Is language the real divider of the 'human
family' and thus the cause of conflict? Visiting
Bialystok without Zamenhof's words limits the city
to being merely an interesting site. Include his words
and there is a discussion to be had, not least because
as a Jew, Zamenhof's optimistic sentiment seems so
tragic when set against the eventual fate of Bialystok,
and indeed European Jewry.

In the first chapter I wrote that the 'voices' of literature offered in this book are a personal selection.
They are literary reflections of journeys between all

the places Jews inhabit; the territory of land and the territory of the mind. I make no claims for creating a canon of Jewish travel literature but rather offer them as a cluster of texts relevant to key locations and contexts. The following have all been chosen for their insight, ability to evoke emotion and provoke thought.

Leaving

Walking and roads bring the journey down to its most basic, the slow progression along the simple lines cut in the earth that define the paths along which we travel. Roads leave the unprotected traveller exposed: to the elements, to unseen dangers and thus to their own fears and insecurities. Roads are perfect settings for Jewish journeys.

Two generations down the Patriarchal line, the Torah offers the dramatic episode of Jacob's flight from his brother Esau. Although different in many ways from Abraham's departure, Jacob's journey was another case of the intermingling of physical and spiritual journeys. In this episode, Jacob takes to the road having been told by both his parents to leave, each for different reasons. His father Isaac, who is close to death, tells him to seek a wife whilst Rebecca warns him of his brother's wrath after taking the birthright. The journey was not his initiative and nor is he leaving in the best of circumstances.

> And Jacob went out [Heb. '*Vayetze*'] from
> Beer Sheva and went towards Haran. And
> he came upon a place and stayed there all
> night. Because the sun had set; and he took
> one of the stones there and put it under
> his head and lay down there to sleep. And
> he dreamed, and there he saw a ladder set
> upon the earth and the top of it reached
> to heaven, and behold the angels of God
> were ascending and descending on it. And
> behold, the Lord God stood beside him and
> said, "I am the Lord, the God of Abraham
> your father, the God of Isaac. The land you
> are standing on I will give to you and your
> descendants. And your descendants shall be
> as the dust of the earth and you shall spread

abroad to the west and to the east, and to the north and the south. And in you and your seed shall all the families of the earth be blessed. And behold I am with you ..."[2]

In these few short lines, the Torah offers a myriad of nuances and suggestions. This is not Abraham's *'lech lecha'* ('go out', or 'go you yourself') but the more straightforward *'vayetze'* ('and he went out'). Earlier, his grandfather Abram left after a single command from God in search of an unknown place. For Abram there was no departure scene and no words of farewell, he simply left. Jacob, on the other hand, was encouraged to leave by his own parents, knowing as they did of the strife between him and his brother. To all intents and purposes he was pushed and not pulled to another place. And so, having departed the family home, the people he knew, and the Land of Israel, Jacob was for the first time on a journey entirely alone, away from all that was known and secure. In fact he was leaving a troubled and broken home, his father dying and his brother wishing to kill him. Maybe it should not be surprising that he behaves as he does on his first day and night away. As the sun goes down, Jacob is found praying, making him the first character in the Torah to seek God in the darkness. This may have been a journey with a physical destination but essentially it was a journey into himself. The dream could not have come at a better time.

In this vulnerable state, Jacob the traveller has a moment of revelation and inspiration in the form of the ladder dream. With its top in heaven and its bottom on earth, he witnesses the journey of the angels, ascending and descending, going away and coming towards him. Why, asks Rashi, the great medieval Hebrew commentator, do the angels ascend before descending? Surely, they would need to come down first before returning to heaven. The answer, says Rashi is all about the place, and by implication about the importance of this journey.

> The angels that accompanied him in the
> Holy Land do not go outside the Holy
> Land. They therefore ascended to Heaven.

Then the angels of outside the Land of
Israel descended to accompany him.[3]

By morning Jacob is a changed man, having discovered that even beyond the boundaries of the Land of
Israel and in spite of his family woes, God is with
him. Despite his leaving, the loss of home with its
warmth and reassurance, Jacob has managed to affirm
the sense of who he is. Only the day before he could
only see the prospect of exile, yet by morning this
had changed. He anointed the spot as '*Beit El*' (lit.
'House of God'), referred to later by commentators as
Mount Moriah, the place where his father Isaac was
not sacrificed by Abraham, the foundation stone of
the world, and the site of the Temple yet to be built.
Jacob's leaving would mark a point of arrival.

Jaffa
Most journeys, including literary ones, begin from
home.

In my case this is not difficult since Jerusalem
is overflowing with journey dramas. Abraham for

instance, did not sacrifice his son that far from my house, on Mount Moriah. There is hardly a stone in Jerusalem that has not been turned over by an archaeologist looking for words to prove someone or other's existence. The desire of contemporary Israelis to discover themselves in the archaeology of the city can be impressive at times, even exciting, but only up to a point. Therefore, I wish to ignore Jerusalem for a moment and choose a different location in Israel to start the journey.

Standing by the site of the port of Jaffa, the ancient entry and departure point from the Land of Israel, I imagine the reluctant prophet Jonah as a pale, worried-looking man deciding which ship to board. Along with God Jonah is the chief protagonist in one of the finest pieces of Biblical travel literature to be found. At one point, he goes on board and disappears into himself. Despite the reading of Jonah as an allegorical tale presenting themes of atonement and responsibility, it also reveals the drama of a man on a journey.

Now the word of the Lord came to Jonah
the son of Amittai, saying, Arise, go to
Nineveh, that great city, and cry against
it; for their wickedness is come up before
me. But Jonah rose up to flee to Tarshish
from the presence of the Lord, and went
down to Jaffa; and he found a ship going to
Tarshish: so he paid the fare of it, and went
down into it, to go with them to Tarshish
from the presence of the Lord. But the
Lord hurled a great wind upon the sea, and
there was a mighty tempest in the sea, so
that the ship seemed likely to be wrecked.
Then the mariners were afraid, and cried
every man to his god, and threw out the
articles that were in the ship into the sea,
to lighten it for them. But Jonah was gone
down into the recesses of the ship; and
he lay down, and was fast asleep. So the
shipmaster came to him, and said to him,
What meanest thou, O sleeper? Arise; call
upon thy God, perhaps God will think

upon us, that we perish not. And they
said everyone to his fellow, Come, and let
us cast lots, that we may know for whose
cause this evil is upon us. So they cast lots,
and the lot fell upon Jonah. Then they said
to him, "Tell us, we pray you, for whose
cause this evil is upon us; what is your
occupation? and where do you come from?
what is your country? and of what people
do you belong?" And he said to them, I am
a Hebrew; and I fear the Lord, the God of
heaven, who made the sea and the dry land.

Now the Lord had appointed a great
fish to swallow up Jonah. And Jonah was
in the belly of the fish for three days and
three nights. Then Jonah prayed to the
Lord his God out of the fish's belly, and
said, I cried to the Lord out of my distress,
and he heard me; out of the belly of She'ol
I cried and thou didst hear my voice. For
thou didst cast me into the deep, into the
heart of the seas; and the floods corn passed

me about: all thy billows and thy waves passed over me. Then I said, I am cast out of thy sight; yet I will look again towards thy holy temple. The waters compassed me about, to the point of death: the depth closed me round about; the weeds were wrapped about my head. I went down to the bottoms of the mountains; the earth with her bars closed on me forever: yet hast thou brought up my life from the pit, O Lord my God. When my soul fainted within me I remembered the Lord: and my prayer came in to thee, into thy holy temple. They that guard lying vanities forsake their loyalty. But I will sacrifice to thee with the voice of thanksgiving; I will pay that which I have vowed. Salvation belongs to the Lord.

And the Lord spoke to the fish, and it vomited out Jonah upon the dry land. And the word of the Lord came to Jonah the second time, saying, Arise, go to Nineveh,

that great city, and proclaim to it the message that I bid thee. So Jonah arose, and
went to Nineveh, according to the word of
the Lord.[4]

When God calls Jonah he runs in the opposite
direction. Maybe he is a reluctant traveller, preferring
not to move beyond his existing reality? After all,
why would he want to travel to Nineveh, the capital
of the hated Assyrians who had recently conquered
the northern Kingdom of Israel, and offer them the
chance of repentance? Maybe he cannot face the possibility of their potential change? Scared of confronting one path he chooses another, which unknowingly
always returns to the same point; himself.

Throughout, one question keeps returning: where
was Jonah actually travelling to? Is he going towards
or going away from? Away from Nineveh (God,
responsibility, etc) and towards Tarshish (himself,
denial of responsibility)? Towards a confident version
of himself (amongst the other passengers on board the
ship) or away from his true self (hidden down below)?

In all cases, he can never truly run away, evidenced by the powerful dialogue with the sailors in which he finally confronts himself, 'I am a Hebrew'. This is a rich illustration of one of the basic truths of the travel experience; that the direction of most journeys ends up with the self, and thus Jonah's futile flight can only end in failure. The sailors play an impressive role in this process by posing all the questions of identity (What is your occupation? And where do you come from? What is your country? And of what people do you belong?, etc).

The strength of this process is illustrated no less clearly in the dramatic outbursts by the prophet when he is finally forced to see things as they are. Jonah's declaration of identity to the sailors, 'I am a Hebrew', is a deep and pained outburst, followed quickly by a full confession and explanation of the implications of what that means. Strangely, having done such a bad job of running away, Jonah makes a far better go of returning, including his deep felt prayer in the belly of the fish. This is a book with a set of truly remarkable locations: the ship; the belly of the fish; dry land.

Each provides the setting for a different confrontation up to the book's strange climax, when it ends abruptly with Jonah sitting beneath a withered plant in Nineveh, a long way from home and arguing with God.

Rome

The drama of Jaffa is to be found in the sea, a point of departing and arriving. It transcends history. In its own way, the 'eternal city' of Rome does something similar, although when viewed through Jewish eyes many things change. The rabbis of the Talmud decided to write the history of the city by revisiting a previous moment of time.

> Rab Judah said in Samuel's name: When
> Solomon married Pharaoh's daughter,
> Gabriel descended and planted a reed in
> the sea and around gathered around it, on
> which the great city of Rome was built ...[5]

Intermarriage between Hebrew kings and gentile

princesses was frowned upon by the rabbis, which seemed a fair way to denigrate the capital of the powerful and pagan regime. This was a literary blow in the cultural war between two competing civilisations, between advocates of flesh versus spirit.

Eternal or not, Rome is home to the oldest Jewish community in Europe, stretching back over 2,000 years. How does one develop this symbol of antiquity in words? A late nineteenth-century Roman Jewish writer, in the first years following emancipation from the ghetto offers the following observation.

> Twenty centuries have passed and only
> a few ruins remain of what was imperial
> Rome, and of the immortal gods nothing
> but the odd vague image; of the glory, the
> power and the innumerable treasures only
> a pale memory remains. Patricians, plebs,
> consuls, emperors, masters of the world
> passed leaving hardly a trace, yet the sons
> of the Jews, slaves of Pompey and Titus,
> still survive. They have seen fall to dust

around them the ancient Roman Republic,
the Kingdom of the Caesars, Byzantium
and the conquests of the Barbarians,
the anarchy of the Middle Ages and the
dominion of the Pope; they, however live
on. It is fifteen centuries since the fall
of the proud image of Capitoline Jove,
which had seemed to be eternal, but by the
Capitoline hill the Jewish rite has remained
immobile and unchanged.[6]

There is no neutrality when it comes to Rome, as the
capital of civilisations and empires with records of
brutality and oppression in relation to Jews. Ancient
Rome destroyed Jewish independence in the Land of
Israel, the Roman Church embittered the lives of Jews
throughout the Middle Ages, bequeathing a legacy of
humiliation and ghettoisation up to the dawn of the
modern world. And yet, the Jews of Rome survive,
quietly hinting at a different truth, that power and
empire do not guarantee survival.

Yet, there are other symbols in Rome, to be found

at specific locations, complete with words to be read at them. I would dearly love to insert the following passage from the Talmud in the guidebooks sold outside the Coliseum. It could be read alongside the paeans to its architectural triumph.

> Our Rabbis taught: Those who visit
> stadiums and camps and witness there the
> performance of sorcerers and enchanters
> … against those who visit them, the
> Scripture says, "Happy is the man that has
> not walked in the counsel of the wicked …
> nor sat in the seat of the scornful, but his
> delight is in the Law of the Lord". From
> here you can infer that those things cause
> one to neglect the Torah.
>
> The following was cited as
> contradicting the forgoing: It is permitted
> to go to stadiums, because by shouting one
> may save the victim. The laws relating to
> stadiums are surely contradictory! They
> represent the differing opinions of two

Tannaim [rabbis of the Mishna]. For it
has been taught: One should not go to
stadiums because they are "the seat of the
scornful", but R. Nathan permits it for
two reasons: first, because by shouting one
may be able to save the victim, secondly,
because one might be able to give evidence
of death for the wife and enable her to
remarry.

It is forbidden to go to the
amphitheatre of gentiles, because of
idolatry, so says Rabbi Meir, but the
Sages say, when they offer sacrifices it
is forbidden because it is "feat of the
scornful" (Psalm 1:1-2). One who goes
to the amphitheatre so as to shout for
mercy, if it is for their public welfare, it
is permitted, but if he associates with
them, it is forbidden. One who sits in
the amphitheatre is guilty of bloodshed.
Rabbi Nathan permits it because of two
considerations. As a spectator he may shout

for mercy and thus save lives, and he may
be able to testify so as to enable a woman
to remarry.[7]

This is truly a literature of 'place'! Is it permissible, ask the rabbis, for Jews to visit the place where public sport is made of killing? As the central arena for public sport and entertainment, including gladiatorial contests and fighting with wild animals, this is a site that speaks of the deep culture-clash between Roman and Jewish civilisations. Tourism and morality face off against each other in a weighty commentary on the act of witnessing: 'One who sits in the amphitheatre is guilty of bloodshed,' and 'As a spectator he may shout for mercy and thus save lives'.

Moving to the streets of the modern city, the symbols do not lighten up and the themes do not change. In 1553, Romans no longer had to endure the corrupting presence of Jews on their streets as they were shut up in the ghetto. In that same year, hundreds of copies of the Talmud were burnt in the Campo di Fiore (lit. 'Field of Flowers'). Today a statue in the

Campo di Fiore witnesses a different burning, that of the philosopher Giordano Bruno, executed by the dark forces of the Counter-Reformation. Suddenly, in this most beautiful of Rome's piazzas, a voice emerges in the poem of Czeslaw Milosz, written in Warsaw in 1943, many years before he would become a Nobel Prize laureate. The power of witnessing returns to the fore as the poet sees across the ages, caught up in the drama of history.

> *Here, on this very square*
> *Giordano Bruno was burned:*
> *The hangmen kindled the flame of the pyre*
> *In the ring of the gaping crowd,*
> *And hardly the flame extinguished*
> *The taverns were full again*
> *And hawkers carried on heads*
> *Baskets with olives and lemons.*
>
> *I recalled Campo di Fiore*
> *In Warsaw, on a merry-go-round,*
> *On a fair night in the spring*

> *By the sound of vivacious music.*
> *The salvoes behind the ghetto walls*
> *Were drowned in lively tunes,*
> *And vapours freely rose*
> *Into the tranquil sky* ...[8]

Suddenly Rome, Giordano Bruno and the Campo di Fiore come together and are joined to the spirit of the Talmud. Czeslaw Milosz rode the tram by the walls of the Warsaw ghetto as it went up in flames and its inhabitants were killed. For him, seeing meant speaking, bearing witness to the injustice. His poem was published in 1944 in a Polish underground anthology 'From the Abyss' dedicated to the Jewish victims. Ultimately, he declared, it is the poet's mission to recall the world's forgotten victims in a protest against the re-occurrence of tyranny.

Damascus/Baghdad

I have never been to Damascus or Baghdad nor am I likely to in the near future. Political circumstances do not permit such journeys, thereby ensuring these two cities remain firmly in the present and disallowing any engagement with their magnificent pasts. It falls to the great Jewish traveller of the Middle Ages, Benjamin of Tudela, to make the necessary connections.

For reasons unknown, Benjamin departed from his home in northern Spain in 1159 and travelled along the southern French coast down into Italy. From there he went to Corfu, Constantinople, Cyprus, Palestine, Damascus and onwards to Baghdad and Persia. The final leg took him to India and possibly to China! Little is known of the dashing Benjamin of Tudela except whatever can be deduced from his extensive travelogue.

> This is the book of travels, which was
> compiled by Rabbi Benjamin, the son of
> Jonah of the land of Navarre. His repose
> be in Paradise! The said Rabbi Benjamin
> set forth from Tudela his native city and
> passed through many remote countries as is
> related in his book …

...Damascus, the great city, which is the commencement of the empire of Nur-al-din, the king of the Togarmin, called Turks. It is a fair city of large extent, surrounded by walls, with many gardens and plantations, extending over fifteen miles on each side, and no district richer in fruit can be seen in all the world. From Mount Hermon descend the rivers Amana and Pharpar; for the city is situated at the foot of Mount Hermon. The Amana flows through the city, and by means of aqueducts the water is conveyed to the houses of great people, and into the streets and market places. The Pharpar flows through their gardens and plantations. It is a place carrying on trade with all countries. Here is a mosque of the Arabs called the Gami of Damascus; there is no building like it in the whole world, and they say that is was a palace of Ben Hadad. Here is a wall of crystal glass of magic workmanship,

with apertures according to the days of
the year, and as the sun's rays enter each of
them in daily succession the hours of the
day can be told by a graduated dial. In the
palace are chambers built of gold and glass,
and if the people walk around the wall
is between them. And there are columns
overlaid with gold and silver, and columns
of marble of all colours ... Three thousand
Jews abide in this city, and amongst them
are learned and rich men.

Baghdad, the great city and royal
residence of the Caliph (Mustanjid) Al
Abbassi of the family of Mohammed. He is
at the head of the Mohammedan religion,
and all the kings of Islam obey him; he
occupies a similar position to that held by
the Pope over Christians ...

There the great king, Al Abbassi the
Caliph (Haft) holds his court, and he is
kind unto Israel, and many belonging to
the people of Israel are his attendants; he

knows all languages, and is well versed
in the law of Israel. He reads and writes
the holy language (Hebrew). He will not
partake of anything unless he has earned
it by the work of his own hands ... He is
truthful and trusty, speaking peace to all
men.

In Baghdad there are about 40,000
Jews, and they dwell in security, prosperity
and honour under the great Caliph;
and amongst them are the great sages,
the heads of Academies engaged in the
study of the law. In this city there are
ten Academies. At the head of the great
Academy is the chief rabbi., R. Samuel, the
son of Eli ... And at the head of them all
[the leaders of the community] is Daniel
the son of Hisdai, who is styled 'Our Lord,
the Head of the Captivity of all Israel'. He
possesses a book of pedigrees going back as
far as David, King of Israel.

... In Baghdad there are 28

synagogues, situated either in the city itself
of in Al-Karish on the other side of the
Tigris; for the river divides the metropolis
in two parts.[9]

Benjamin, the great Jewish adventurer, reminds the
present-day reader of the beauty and splendour of
Damascus. He is not disinterested in the Jews, but
that does not obscure his ability to appreciate everything else. In Baghdad meanwhile, the contemporary reader is reminded that Jews and Muslims lived
well together and that the centre of the Jewish world
was once in the great city of Baghdad. This was in
fact a transition-point in Jewish history as the great
academy receded in greatness surrendering to the new
centres in Spain and Germany.

Jerusalem/Girona/Toledo
I wonder how often Benjamin of Tudela's eyes changed
direction? How often did he look back? Journeys are
often mistakenly assumed to be one-directional, with
little consideration of where one has come from or

where one returns to. The most common journey of the Middle Ages was that of flight, the end product of expulsion or persecution. But for those who chose their journeys, it was the pull of somewhere else, looking towards a destination, invariably Jerusalem. Therefore it seems a little subversive to speculate whether anyone ever looked backwards from this city, regarding it as a point of departure and not destination? Built of stone and the object of prayers and dreams, Jerusalem always seems to be about certainty. Without wishing to undermine the dreams, I must confess, I am more confident with the lack of certainty.

In the late 1260s, Rabbi Moses ben Nahman, the great leader of thirteenth-century Spanish Jewry, arrived in Jerusalem having fled Spain fearing arrest by the Christian authorities. In 1263 he had been obliged to participate in an anti-Jewish show trial, known as a 'disputation', after which he returned to his home in Girona, only to discover shortly thereafter he was being accused of blasphemy. Writing from Jerusalem to his son in Girona, he offered the following reflection on his journey.

A mournful sight I have perceived in thee, Jerusalem. Only one Jew is here, a dyer, persecuted, oppressed, and despised At his house gather great and small when they can get a *minyan*. They are wretched folk, without occupation and trade, consisting of a few pilgrims and beggars, though the fruit of the land is still magnificent and the harvests rich. Indeed it is still a blessed country, flowing with milk and honey ...

Oh! I am a man who has seen affliction. I am banished from my table, removed far away from friend and kinsman, and too long is the distance for me to meet them again ... I left my family. I forsook my house. And there with my sons and daughters, and with the sweet and dear children whom I have brought up on my knees, I left also my soul. My heart and my eyes will dwell with them forever ... But the loss of all this and of every other glory my eyes saw is compensated by having

now the joy of being a day in thy courts, O
Jerusalem, visiting the ruins of the Temple,
and crying over the desolate sanctuary;
where I am permitted to caress thy stones,
to fondle thy dust, and to weep over thy
ruins. I wept bitterly, but I found joy in
my tears. I tore my garments, but I felt
relieved by it.[10]

His words are touching, but I wish to challenge him.
Far away from Jerusalem along the dark yet captivating alleyway known as Carrer de la Forca, in the old
town of Girona (northern Spain), there hides a firm
indentation in the stone by a doorway. Over 500 years
since the expulsion of the Jews from the city, it still
hints at the one time presence of a *mezuzah,* which was
the likely home of Nahmanides. Was he thinking of
this spot when he wrote to his son? Did Jerusalem sink
a little as he thought of that spot? Did he really mean
'But the loss of all this [family] and of every other glory
my eyes saw is compensated by having now the joy of
being a day in thy courts, O Jerusalem ...'

In going back to Jerusalem, the famous words of Yehuda Halevi come to mind, 'My heart is in the East and I am in the depths of the West'. Born in twelfth century Toledo, Yehuda Halevi was a doctor by profession, and enjoyed much of the final years of the 'golden age' of Spanish Jewry. He seemed to have lived much of his life in a state of tension, caught between two places.

> My body is a room where a heart dwells
> That is bound to the wings of an eagle. Can it conquer
> A man weary of life, whose whole desire
> Is to smother his cheeks in the most precious of dusts?
> He trembles. His tears begin to fall.
> He fears to leave Spain, to travel through the world,
> To board a ship, to cross the desert,
> By the lion's den and the leopard's mountain lair.
> He rebukes his friends and decides to go.
> He leaves his house and lives in the wasteland ...
> He will go up to the hills and down to the valleys,
> To fulfil his oath, and to complete his vows.[11]

After much deliberation, Halevi finally left, leaving only his poems as explanation and fresh reflections on home. Whilst at sea, or possibly after landing in Alexandria, he wrote a poem 'The Poet Remembers his Home' in which he expresses his haste and eagerness for this journey, for God and the land.

> I never stopped to kiss my wife,
> My children, friends of kin.
> I shall not weep for the orchard I planted ...
>
> I am finished, now and forever, with creeping ...
> I am making my way through the heart of the sea
> To the place where God's own feet find rest,
> Where I can pour out my soul and my sorrow.[12]

Maybe this is self-justification and/or religious rapture, but these sentiments belong to Jerusalem. At times they are inspiring but they are also unsettling, pitting values of one place against each other. The contemporary Jerusalem poet Yehuda Amichai catches the essence of Jerusalem's dilemma in 'Ecology of Jerusalem'.

> *The air over Jerusalem is saturated with prayers*
>   *and dreams*
> *Like the air over industrial cities ...*
>
> *And from time to time a new shipment of history*
>   *arrives ...*[13]

Naples/Venice

On 24 December 1502, the remarkable Jewish courtier Don Isaac Abravanel presented himself before the Council of Ten in the Palazzo Ducale, the seat of Venetian government. Outwardly, he was offering the councilors of this seafaring city-state a diplomatic plan to protect their economy. On a different level, this was a speech of a man whose life had been characterized by journeys of escape and departure. Recently expelled from Spain, it was the last stage in his search for a home for him and his fellow Jews.

After a period as chief financier to King Alfonso

V of Portugal, he departed swiftly in 1483 when the political wind changed direction, settling in the Castilian capital Toledo, at the court of Ferdinand and Isabella. Not long after, however, disaster struck with the final conquest of Muslim Granada and the subsequent expulsion of Jews from Spain in 1492. To the very end, Abravanel remained, lobbying for clemency and offering financial inducements for rescinding the edict of expulsion. When there was nothing left to be done, Abravanel left, this time together with the thousands of Spanish Jews forced to seek shelter on foreign shores. He travelled to Naples before eventually settling in Venice.

This was the journey of a group, tens of thousands in fact, wedded together by a common experience of success in one of the high points of Jewish diaspora life. From the summer of 1492, they set sail, often penniless hoping for assistance from an active Sephardi diaspora help network. Abravanel's description of the journey of departure is powerful and moving with faintly Biblical overtones.

He [Ferdinand] commanded that the children of Israel could remain in the country only if they submitted to baptism; but if they were unwilling to embrace the Christian faith, they must leave the territories of Spain, Sicily, Majorca and Sardinia. "Within three months," he decreed, "there must not remain in my kingdoms a single Jew."

When the dreadful news reached the people, they mourned their fate and wherever the report of decrees spread, Jews wept bitterly. The terror and lamentation were greater than at any time since the expulsion of our forefathers from their own soil in Judah to foreign lands. However, they encouraged each other bravely; saying "Let us cling unflinchingly to our faith, holding our heads with pride before the voice of the enemy that taunts and blasphemes. If they let us live, we will live; if they kill us, we will perish. But we will

not break our Divine Commandment nor
shall we turn back. We will go forth in the
name of the Lord our God."

With strong resolve, people both young
and old, a multitude of 300,000 from
every province, left one day unarmed and
on foot. I was among them. They went
whithersoever the wind carried them. Some
fled to the Kingdom of Portugal, others
to the Kingdom of Navarre. Many chose
the way of the sea and were lost, drowned,
burnt to death and sold into slavery.
They suffered the curses written in our
Scriptures: "The Lord will cause them to
be smitten before their enemies; they shall
flee seven ways before them; thou shalt be
a horror to all the kingdoms of the earth."
Of this vast host only a small number
survived. Blessed be the Name of the Lord.

I, too, chose the path of my people,
departing on a sea going vessel. I went
into exile with my entire family and came

to this glorious city of Naples whose
kings are merciful. Thereupon I decided
to pay my vow to God by setting upon
the task of writing a commentary on the
book of Kings. It was a time to recall the
destruction of our Holy Temple and the
Exile of our people, all of which are recorded
in this book. It was time to remember our
glories and our misfortunes.[14]

Abravanel was a remarkable man, constantly moving
and it seems always in contact with the various parts
of the new Sephardi Diaspora. He appears unbeaten
yet still searching for security but not despairing.

Berlin

For many Jews, Berlin is not a city they are able to
visit. The weight of memory and symbol is just too
great. Those that do often fret about their ability to
enjoy its liveliness and vitality for fear of offending the
dead. Others enjoy the liberating feeling of knowing
it is a city that has somehow acknowledged its past

sins and tried to make amends. There is nothing neutral about being a Jew in Berlin.

Physically, it is a city that in theory at least, confronts its past in the process of building its future since there can be no construction without acknowledging what was once there. Yet in her outstanding biography of the city, Alexandra Richie draws attention to the other spaces,

> But above all history is in the empty
> spaces – in the broad, windswept fields
> and vacant lots which still stretch across
> the centre of town, where one can still find
> pieces of wrought iron or porcelain from
> long forgotten staircases or dinner services.
> History is there in the single houses which
> stand alone ... History twists through
> the branches of the trees which follow
> abandoned streets and along rusty tram
> tracks leading nowhere ... In Berlin the
> wounds of a troubled past are still painfully
> open, the scars still fresh.[15]

I recall the experience of an Israeli woman of my generation explaining to her grandmother that she had visited Berlin. In reply, the elderly lady, who had left the city in the 1930s, recalled her former home in the predominantly Jewish suburb of Mitte. She emphasised its location opposite the Jewish cemetery on Gross Hamburger Street. The young woman simply could not tell her grandmother that the cemetery had been destroyed by the Nazis and is now a park. In her mind, the elderly woman had not conceived of such destruction. It is precisely the history found in Richie's 'empty spaces'.

Possibly a harder Jewish journey to Berlin is the one that goes back beyond the twentieth century, to a better time since the contrasts are too stark. As in Jacob Glatstein's poem 'Goodnight, World' in the previous chapter, the contrasts only create a counter-reaction. Personally, I refuse to surrender the Berlin to the destructive twentieth century and wish to retain the other city, the one that spoke of Enlightenment and modernity. Therefore as a guide, I choose to read from the memoir of Solomon Maimon, a restless and precocious young Talmud scholar who came to Berlin from Poland at the end of the eighteenth century. Unconvinced of the truths of traditional Orthodoxy, Maimon's desperate journey to Berlin in search of enlightenment represents a moment of geographic and philosophical transition.

My external circumstances were steadily
becoming worse. I was unwilling to adapt
myself to my ordinary occupations any
longer, and hence found myself everywhere
out of my sphere. On the other hand,
my town afforded little means to satisfy
my yearning for study of the sciences.
And I determined to betake myself to
Germany, there to study medicine and,
as opportunity offered, other sciences as
well. But the question was, how so long a
journey was to be made. I knew indeed that
certain merchants of my town were soon to
make a journey to Koenigsberg in Prussia;
my acquaintance with them was slight and

I could not expect that they would take me with them gratis. After much deliberation I hit upon a capital expedient at last.

Among my friends there was a very learned and devout man, who enjoyed great esteem among all the Jews of the town. I revealed my purpose to him, and solicited his counsel. He went to a merchant of his acquaintance, represented to him the importance of my undertaking, and persuaded him to take me with him to Koenigsberg on his own vessel. The merchant could refuse nothing to so godly a man, and so gave his consent.

Accordingly, I set out with this Jewish merchant for Koenigsberg in Prussia. When I arrived there, I went to the Jewish medical doctor of the place, broached my proposal to study medicine, and begged his advice and support. As his professional preoccupations prevented him from conveniently speaking with me on the subject, and as he could not in any case understand me well, he referred me to certain students who lodged in his house. As soon as I showed myself to these young gentlemen, and revealed my intentions, they burst into loud laughter. And certainly they were not to be blamed. Imagine a man from Polish Lithuania of about five-and-twenty years, with a tolerably stiff beard, in tattered dirty clothes, whose language is a mixture of Hebrew, Yiddish, Polish, and Russian, with their several grammatical inaccuracies, who gives it out that he understands the German language, and that he has attained some knowledge of the sciences. What were the young gentlemen to think?

They began to poke fun at me, and gave me Mendelssohn's *Phaedon* to read, which by chance lay on the table. My reading was pitiful, both on account of the peculiar manner in which I had learned

212

the German language, and on account of
my bad pronunciation. Again they burst
into loud laughter; but said I must explain
what I had read. This I did in my own
fashion; but as they did not understand
me, they demanded that I should translate
what I had read into Hebrew. This I
did on the spot. The students, who
understood Hebrew well, fell into no slight
astonishment when they saw that I had
not only grasped correctly the meaning of
this celebrated author, but also expressed
it happily in Hebrew. They then began to
take interest in my welfare, and procured
me cast-off clothing and board during my
stay in Koenigsberg. At the same time they
advised me to go to Berlin, where I should
best attain my object.

And so I went by ship, having no food
except dry biscuit, some herring, and a
flask of spirits. In Koenigsberg I had been
told that the journey might take ten or at

the most fourteen days. But this prognosis was wrong. By reason of contrary winds the voyage lasted five weeks. My state may be easily imagined. There were no other passengers on the vessel but an old woman, who sang hymns all the time for solace. The Pomeranian German of the crew I could understand as little as they could my medley of Yiddish, Polish, and Lithuanian. I got nothing warm to eat the whole time, and was obliged to sleep on hard stuffed bags. On occasion the vessel was near foundering. Of course I was seasick most of the time.

At last I arrived at Stettin, whence I had been told I could easily make the journey to Frankfort on foot. But how was a Polish Jew in the most wretched circumstances, without a penny for food and without knowing the language of the country, to make a journey even of a few miles? Yet it had to be done. Accordingly, I set out from Stettin, and as I thought over

my miserable situation, I sat down under
a lime tree, and began to weep bitterly.
My spirit soon became somewhat lighter;
I took courage, and went on. After I had
gone some miles, I arrived towards evening
at an inn, quite exhausted. It was the eve
of the Jewish fast which falls in August.
Already I was nearly starving with hunger
and thirst, and I was still to fast the whole
of the next day. I had not a penny to spend
and nothing of any value to sell.

After long reflection it occurred to me
that I must still have in my coat pocket an
iron spoon, which I had taken with me on
board ship. I brought it, and begged the
landlady of the inn to give me a little bread
and beer for it. At first she refused to take
the spoon, but after much importunity she
was at last induced to grant a glass of sour
beer in exchange. I was obliged to content
myself with this, drank my glass of beer,
and went off to the stable to sleep on straw.

In the morning I proceeded on my
journey, having previously inquired for
a place where Jews were to be found, so
that I might be able to go to synagogue,
and join with my brethren in chanting
the lamentations over the destruction
of Jerusalem. This was done, and after
the prayers and singing, about midday,
I went to the Jewish schoolmaster of the
place, and had some conversation with
him. He soon discovered that I was a full
rabbi, began to interest himself in my
case, and procured me a supper at the
house of a Jew. He also gave me a letter of
introduction to another schoolmaster in the
neighbouring town, recommending me as
a great Talmudist and an honourable rabbi.
Here also I met with a fair reception. I was
invited to the Sabbath dinner by the most
respectable and richest Jew of the place,
and went into the synagogue, where I was
shown to the choicest pew, and received

every mark of honour usually bestowed on a rabbi.

After the close of the service the rich Jew referred to took me to his house, and put me in the place of honour at his table, that is, between himself and his daughter. She was a young girl of about twelve years, dressed in the most beautiful style. I began, as rabbi, to hold a very learned and edifying discourse; and the less the gentleman and lady understood it, the more divine it seemed to them. All at once I observed, to my chagrin, that the young lady began to put on a sour look, and to make wry faces. At first I did not know how to explain this; but, after a while, when I turned my eyes upon myself and my miserable dirty suit of rags, the whole mystery was at once unriddled. The uneasiness of the young lady had a very good cause. And how could it be otherwise? Since I left Koenigsberg,

about seven weeks before, I had never had
a clean shirt to put on; and I had been
obliged to lie in the stables of inns on bare
straw, on which who knows how many
poor travellers had lain before. Now all at
once I realized my misery in its appalling
magnitude. But what was I to do? How
was I to help myself out of this unfortunate
situation? Gloomy and sad, I soon bade
farewell to these good people, and proceeded on my journey to Berlin, struggling
continually with want and misery of every
kind.[16]

The journey of Solomon Maimon with his account of
privation and hardship makes for gripping reading. In
the end enlightenment wins out as Maimon settles in
Berlin and finds Moses Mendelssohn and Immanuel
Kant. Symbolically, this is a powerful image for the
city, as a bright Polish Jew surrenders the traditional
world for the bright new world of modernity.

It is all the more challenging then to read this

passage in the park on Gross Hamburger Street whose only grave is a symbolic marker; that of Moses Mendelssohn. Elsewhere in the city, one can look down at other empty spaces; the railway sidings seen from the Putlitzbrucke or on the platform at Grunewald Station where the Jewish inheritors of the modern world were deported as cattle. Maybe it is fair to say that Berlin is only visitable as a Jew if one is willing to grapple with the seemingly irreconcilable tensions of the past.

Paris

Joseph Roth's post-First World War non-fiction work *The Wandering Jews* is a masterpiece of modern Jewish travel literature. His subjects are the Eastern European Jews displaced by the war, living in the capital cities of the West, whilst the author himself is an itinerant Jewish journalist and author, wedded to the fate of his subjects.

The Wandering Jews was written in the light of Roth's numerous encounters in Europe as a war correspondent witnessing the uprooting and ensuing

hardship foisted upon Jews on the European bor-
derlands to the east. It is a rich work, literally
overflowing with observations and 'adoring
portraits and analyses' of people rooted in a culture
dissonant with the one they found themselves in.
Significantly he appears to have contempt for the
rooted Jews of the West who he regards as self-
serving assimilationists.

PARIS

It wasn't easy for Eastern Jews to make
their way to Paris. Brussels and Amsterdam
were both far more obvious destinations.
The Jewish gem trade goes to Amsterdam.
A few reduced and a few aspiring Jewish
gem dealers found themselves compelled to
remain on French-speaking territory.

The little Eastern Jew has a somewhat
exaggerated fear of a completely foreign
language. German is almost a mother
tongue to him: he would far rather go to
Germany than France. The Eastern Jew

has a wonderful ear for foreign languages, but his pronunciation is never perfect. It is always possible to pick him out. It's a sound instinct on his part that warns him against the Romance languages.

But even sound instincts may be mistaken. Eastern Jews live almost as well in Paris as God in France (a play on the German proverb *wie Gott in Frankreich,* meaning "to live well" or "off the fat of the land").

No one prevents them from having their own businesses, and there are even whole ghettoes here. There are several Jewish quarters in Paris, around Montmartre and close to the Bastille. They are some of the oldest parts of Paris. They are some of the oldest buildings in Paris, with some of the lowest rents. Unless they are very rich, Jews do not like spending their money on "pointless" luxuries.

There are some quite superficial reasons

why it should be easier for them in Paris. Their faces do not give them away. Their vivacity does not attract notice. Their sense of humour meets that of the French part way. Paris is a real metropolis. Vienna used to be one. Berlin will one day become one. A real metropolis is objective. Of course it has its prejudices too, but no time to indulge them. In the Vienna Prater there is almost no hint of anti-Semitism, in spite of the fact that not all the visitors are fond of Jews, and they find themselves cheek by jowl with some of the most Eastern of Eastern Jews. And why not? Because people enjoy themselves in the Prater. In the Taborstrasse, on the way back from the Prater, the anti-Semite begins to feel anti-Semitic again. There's no fun to be had on the Taborstrasse.

There's no fun in Berlin. But fun rules in Paris. In Paris crude anti-Semitism is confined to the joyless, to the royalists,

the group around the *Action française*. I am
not surprised that the royalists are without
influence in France, and will remain so.
They are not French enough. They have too
much pathos and not enough irony.

Paris is objective, though objectivity
may be a German virtue. Paris is
democratic. The German perhaps has
warmth. But in Paris there is a great
tradition of practical humanity. Paris is
where the Eastern Jew begins to become a
Western European. He becomes French. He
may even come to be a French patriot.

In Paris I visited the Yiddish Theater
Strollers were left in the cloakroom.
Umbrellas were taken into the theater. The
stalls were full of mothers and infants. The
seats were not set in rows; they could be
moved around. People wandered up and
down the side aisles. One person left his
seat, someone else sat down in it. People
ate oranges, which squirted aromatically.

They spoke aloud, sang along, applauded
in midscene. The young Jewish women
spoke only French. They were as elegant
as Parisiennes. They were beautiful. One
might have taken them for women from
Marseilles. They have Parisian gifts. They
are cool and flirtatious. They are gay
and matter-of-fact. They are as faithful
as Parisian women. The assimilation of
a people always begins with the women.
The play was a comedy in three acts. In
the first act the Jewish family in a small
Russian village wants to emigrate. In the
second they get their passports. In the
third, the family is in America and has
become rich and vulgar. They are in the
process of forgetting their former home
and their old friends, who have followed
them to America. The play offers plenty
of opportunities for singing American
hit songs and old Russian-Yiddish songs.
When the Russian songs and dances were

put on, the actors and the audience wept. If it had been just the actors, it would have been kitschy. But when the audience cried too, it was genuinely sad. Jews are easily moved – I knew that. But I didn't know they could be moved by homesickness.

The relationship between stage and audience was close, almost intimate. For Jews it is a fine thing to be an actor. The director came out and announced the next production. Personally – not in the press, not by posters. He said: "Next Wednesday, you will see Monsieur X. from America." He spoke like a leader to his followers. He spoke plainly and wittily. They understood his jokes. Almost got them in advance. Sniffed the punch line.[17]

For Joseph Roth, the Jews of Eastern Europe are presented as a single group who are defined by their absence from their true homes. Yet, stuck on a journey not of their own making, they manage as best they can. It seems clear that Joseph Roth was part of his own book, a wandering Jew at a critical moment in history. The journey ended for him in 1939 when he collapsed and died upon hearing of the suicide of the Jewish writer Ernst Toller. Toller could not cope with the new Europe and all it represented and by implication it was one tragedy too far for Roth. He was in Paris at the time.

Montreal

Roth's observations were of a people in transition, the East European Jews finding themselves in a new diaspora. It was the latest chapter in a larger journey that saw the transformation (in some senses a dissolution) of a unique civilisation. Across the world, East European Ashkenaz transplanted itself and set about re-establishing its institutions, at times successfully but often less so. I remember the thrill of attending a public forum in Winnipeg to discuss the future of Yiddish in the city. I had not read my cultural map properly, naturally expecting the meeting to be in translation and was amazed that not only was it conducted in Yiddish, but the average age was closer to 50 and not 80. Several days later I visited the current incarnation of another of those institutions of the immigrant cultural pioneers, the Jewish People's Library in Montreal. If Jewish communities are remembered for the institutions they create, one of Montreal's crowning glories must be the Jewish People's Library. Having begun informally in 1903 as the Jewish Library and Reading Room the institution grew to become a statement of cultural ambition, through its formal inauguration as the *Folks Bibiliotek*, the Jewish People's Library in 1914. The inclusion of the word 'People's' in the name of the library already betrays a little of its institutional objective, namely to be a vehicle for the culture of the Jews, the democratic culture of language spoken by all and accessible by all. This was a time when cultural politics were at their height, with the ongoing battles to define to crown Yiddish or Hebrew as *the* national language of the Jews. Sitting in the current reading room, I encountered the words of one of those pioneers, the editor of the Yiddish newspaper *Kenedler Adler*, Yankev Yitzchok Segal.

Korets Landscape

In Korets, my city in Volynia,
there were tall wiry thieves,
I saw them in chains;
Strong, broad, they walked on the road,
and the guards who escorted them
reached to their shoulders.
Were it not for their flashy buttons
and tall hats and dangling swords,
I would have looked away.
The thieves captured in broad daylight
in the church cellar,
who were chased through the cavern
for half a day,
soared with their heads high.
Pigeons flew from the church;
children burst forth from the streets.
I see the tumult now,
though years have passed;
even the priest with blond braid,
chain slung across his back,
followed the crowd.

Their height and their power,
their silence, their gentle smiles,
persist even today.

I say "lehavdl", "lehavdl",
"lehavdl", "lehavdl",
one thousand times,
dividing sacred and profane.
Still, in my mind's eye
are two Korets rabbis;
one old, with a white beard,
the other young with a short blond beard,
both from Lithuania Byelorussia
Everyone in town knew them,
and they met occasionally in the market:
"Good day, Reb Mendel",
"Good day to you, Yisroel",
And they would stand and talk
smoothly, so elegantly
that everyone blessed and cherished them
in reverence
and the summer day was radiant.

I see it now, gleaming from there;
in the market, the noise wanes,
and the old beggar plays piously
on a thin string
near a ditch;
I can hear the sun's golden drone
in its passage across the sky
over the old Korets marketplace.
(translated by Grace Schulman)

My heart sank a little realising that despite the better physical conditions away from Europe, for Segal at least, it was a defeat. He was a man caught between two worlds; something that could never change. The emotional ties that transcend geography and emigration exist throughout Segal's poems. The intensity reaches breaking point in a poem recollecting his wedding ('At My Wedding') as he describes the fiddler playing tuneful laments of the old country. The music evokes memories which in turn create pain, and soon the fiddler has the people transfixed.

It was at my wedding this poor devil played,
No one could stand still, yet all were rooted,
Ears in the air like pointed spears,
While the little fiddle tenderly caressed
And fiercely scored the people,
Tore them to bits, flayed them and drew blood
To all their veins
Until strung as taut as violin strings
The old folk, doddering, cried out for mercy.

(translated by Miriam Waddington)[18]

This is a journey of the imagination. Due to the revellers' memories, longing and nostalgia are part of the performance.

Poland/Krakow

The guide's dilemma: how does one speak at sites of the Holocaust? I acknowledge this may be my dilemma and not one shared by others, but my suspicion is that others feel it too. The Holocaust was a moment of extremity and words are limiting, creating the risk of an improper tourist experience. If standing by the site of a death camp, railway tracks or an emptied village, I cannot truly present the magnitude of what happened so maybe I should just withdraw? In relation to the 'great Auschwitz field', the Polish Jewish poet, Henryk Grynberg in his poem 'Poplars' says the following,

> *I don't try to understand anything*
> *nor say anything*
> *what else can one*
> *have to say here*
>
> *I come here to add my own*
> *to the growing silence*

Grynberg, together with his mother, were the sole survivors of their entire extended family. I am only a tour guide. Some guides bypass the problem by rushing straight to the conclusions, keen to emphasize what they believe the site means. In some cases this can be meaningful, in many cases it sounds crass. I am suspicious since no amount of hyperbole ever seems to transmit the power of the event itself. And yet, words must be spoken, victims must be recalled. Maybe it is the easier option, but the words of the victim often seem more appropriate.

Walking the streets of the beautiful Polish city of Krakow, I am aware of the words of its folk poet and singer Mordechai Gebirtig, who lived there before the war and during the city's ghettoisation in 1940. He was murdered two years later. His words reflect on the journey of departure, away from the city to the ghetto in the run-down suburb of Podgorze.

> ### Farewell, My Kraków (Blayb gezunt mir Kroke!)
>
> *Farewell, my Kraków!*
> *So, I wish you well*
> *The cart is waiting at my house*
> *The wild enemy drives me out*
> *As one drives out a stray dog,*
> *Without mercy, far away from you*
>
> *Farewell, my Kraków!*

Perhaps today for the last time
I will see all that is dear to me
By my mother's grave
My heart cries out in pain
It was never so hard to part from her

My eyes are crying too,
Until I can shed no more tears
The cold gravestone of my father becomes wet with them
And my grandfather's gravestone,
I cannot even find,
It must have turned to sand.

Farewell, my Kraków!
Your earth is holy;
There rest my beloved parents,
To lie with them forever,
Will not be my fate
A grave awaits me elsewhere

Farewell, my Kraków!
So, I wish you well

The cart is waiting at my house
The wild enemy drives me out
As one drives out a stray dog
Without mercy, far away from you
Kraków, 1940 [19]

In his leaving, Gebirtig asserts his identity, beyond that of victim to that of a son, connected by bonds of emotion and love to the place where his parents are buried and mournful at the prospect of meeting death elsewhere. This reflection on departure contrasts so dramatically with the words that can be read along the ubiquitous railway lines that haunt most journeys to Poland.

Over 100 people were packed into our cattle car … it is impossible to describe the tragic situation in our airless, closed car. Everyone tried to push his way to a small air opening. I found a crack in one of the floorboards into which I pushed my nose to get a little air. The stench in the cattle

car was unbearable. People were defecating
in all four corners of the car ... After some
time, the train suddenly stopped. A guard
entered the car. He had come to rob us.
He took everything that had not been
well hidden: money, watches, valuables ...
Water! We pleaded with railroad workers.
We would pay them well ... I paid 500
zlotys and received a cup of water – about
half a litre. As I began to drink, a woman,
whose child had fainted, attacked me. She
was determined to make me leave her a
little water.[20]

The witness speaks in blank words, seemingly devoid
of emotion yet full of terrible power. And then there
is a literature of arrival. By the ramp in Auschwitz-
Birkenau, 60 kilometres from Kraków, I have read the
following words from *Night* by Elie Wiesel.

... We jumped out. I threw a last glance
towards Madame Schachter. Her little boy

was holding her hand. In front of us flames.
In the air that smell of burning flesh. It
must have been about midnight. We had
arrived – at Birkenau, the reception for
Auschwitz ...

   ... that was the moment when I parted
from my mother. I had not had time to
think, but already I felt the pressure of
my father's hand ... For a part of a second
I glimpsed my mother and my sister
moving away to the right. Tzipora held my
mother's hand. I saw them disappear into
the distance; my mother was stroking my
sister's fair hair, as though to protect her,
while I walked on with my father and the
other men. And I did not know that in that
place, at that moment, I was parting from
my mother and Tzipora forever.[21]

Vilna

The Book of Lamentations begins with a reflection on
the destroyed city of Jerusalem,

O how the city that was once so populous
Remained lonely like a widow! She that was
  great amongst the nations
A princess among the provinces, has become a vassal.

The Hebrew name for this lesser-read book of the
Bible is taken from its opening words, *Eichah* meaning
how, which is the overriding question to be asked of
visits to Vilna, the Jerusalem of Lithuania. I confess to
having no objectivity regarding Vilna. This was the
centre of so many innovative movements that define
the modern Jewish world: home of the YIVO (Yiddish
Scientific Institute), the powerhouse of secular Jewish
scholarship; the birthplace of the Jewish revolutionary movement, the Bund and the hub of the Yeshiva
world (the academies of rabbinic scholarship). In the
terms of Lamentations – *Eichah*, how then does one
visit Vilna after the Holocaust, when the Nazis tore
out its heart? It is the very question asked by the
Yiddish poet Avraham Sutzkever in his poem of that
name, as he was living in the ghetto in 1943.

How will you fill your goblet
On the day of liberation? And with what?

How do we return? The answer begins by recalling life – the Vilna before the destruction. On a bench, opposite Vokieciu Street by the site of what was once Velfkeh's (see below), I read to groups from a memoir of Vilna written by Lucy Dawidowicz, who recalled her life there in 1938. Having travelled there from her native New York to Vilna to work as an intern at the YIVO Institute, she met the great and the good of the Yiddish world before fleeing homewards in the last days before the invasion. The two cities were capitals of the Yiddish-speaking world; the former theoretically the newer and the latter part of the 'old world'. Yet all is inverted as she tells of the spontaneity and youthfulness in Vilna's Yiddish scene.

> There was always something going on in
> Vilna – a world-famous Zionist leader came
> to speak; a Yiddish school put on its annual
> children's show; a visiting poet from

Warsaw was feted with a public poetry
reading; the Jewish Symphonic Orchestra
had a concert; a Yiddish theatrical troupe
came for a short run; a Jewish scholar from
Lodz delivered a lecture. These programs,
conducted in Yiddish, usually drew a full
house. My greatest astonishment, at least
in the early months of my stay in Vilna
was that the audience were mostly young
people. In New York, during the 1930s, a
Yiddish lecture, even the Yiddish theatre
drew mainly older people, balding, greying
our parents and grandparents. We of the
Sholem Aleichem Yungt Gezelschaft were
the exception ...

In Vilna things were just the reverse.
Cultural and political events drew a young
and lively audience. To be sure, there were
older people as well, but it was exciting
for me to be with a young generation of
Yiddish speakers. I felt at the centre of
things. Here, I didn't bear the burden of

responsibility for the future of Yiddish. In
Vilna, the world of traditional Judaism, as
I saw it in the *kloyzn* was in the hands of
the old, but the secular culture of Yiddish
belonged to the young.

A few weeks after I had arrived in Vilna
I was introduced to a group whose very
name epitomized the connection between
Yiddish and youth. Called *yung vilne* Young
Vilna, it was an association of writers and
artists of which I had already heard back
in New York. In mid-September, someone
called Shmerke Kaczerginski telephoned
me at the YIVO and introduced himself
as a member of Young Vilna. He'd been
told by a mutual friend in New York to
look me up. He invited me to join him
and his friends that Saturday evening at
a place where Vilna's Yiddish Bohemia
congregated ...

He took me to a place called Velfkeh's
('Wolfie's'), named for its owner Wolf

Ussian. It was, I learned, one of Vilna's famous institutions. Here Vilna's Yiddish writers, actors and intellectuals came to eat and drink, to entertain their out-of-town guests, to celebrate festive occasions and sometimes just to enjoy themselves. In a short time I, too, began to go there frequently. Located in the very heart of the Jewish quarter, on ulica Zydowska (*yidishe gas*), corner of ulica Niemecka (*deutsche gas*), Velfkeh's was unprepossessing on the outside and even more so on the inside. A large Yiddish sign on the street directed you into the courtyard to the restaurant where you could get breakfast, dinner, and supper.

You always saw knots of people outside Velfkeh's, for Vilna's droshky drivers used to stop off there for a drink. As I remember it, Velfkeh's, like Caesar's Gaul, was divided into three parts. You came into a saloon, sawdust on the floor, with

a bar buffet and a bartender. A group of
burly men always congregated at the bar,
drinking, talking, guffawing, swearing
Besides being a watering place for the
droshky drivers, Velfkeh's bar was a
hangout for Vilna's Jewish toughs.

You walked through this entry-room
into a second somewhat larger space,
with about six tables, where you would
sometimes see middle class families who
had come to make a special occasion with a
meal out. Passing through this room, you
came into a place that was at least twice
as wide as it was deep, like a banquet hall.
I remember it as utterly plain, without
attractive lighting or ornamentation. It
was furnished with several long table and
benches and a few smaller tables and chairs.
The floor was bare with space for dancing,
a radio provided the music. The kitchen
was some place off this room. Here you
could be served beer, wine, vodka, or just

tea, if you preferred. You could eat chopped liver and cracklings, gefilte fish, boiled beef, *cholent*, and roast goose. On Hanukkah we came for potato pancakes and on *Shevuot* for cheese blintzes.

Velfkeh took pleasure in his literary-bohemian circle, even if they didn't always have the money to spend. Their presence gave his place a certain cachet in Vilna's Yiddishist circles. Besides, the bohemians were sometimes accompanied by a patron of the arts who picked up the tab.[22]

Today, Velfkeh's is a mirage, or at least a mental image to be conjured up when sitting on the corner of the two streets in central Vilnius. Davidowicz's evocation of that place belongs to a beautiful moment in history. She restores Vilna to its former glory, a place we can never visit, except in the imagination. How does one go back?

Occasional pictures surface in exhibitions and albums showing squares and streets minutes after the

Jews were taken. Suitcases and occasional debris were all that was left as the people were being shot in the nearby forests of Ponar. Sutzkever survived the war in the partisans, yet recalled that last image of the empty street in his post war poem, 'Toys',

> *Love them, your little princesses —*
> *I remember a cursed night*
> *When there were dolls left in all the seven streets*
> *Of the city. And not one child.*

A full account of the journey back to those streets belongs to Chaim Grade who survived the war having fled to Soviet Central Asia. Grade (1910–82) was a member of *Yung Vilne*, a dynamic literary group who frequented Velfkeh's and a writer with a profound sense of 'place'. His places were the Yeshivot (Talmudic academies) of Navardok, connected to the moralist and ethically obsessed community of the Musar movement. After breaking away from this religious world, he gravitated to his other place, Vilna. His return generates deep and indescribable pain, a reaction proportionate to the deep love that had once connected him to Vilna. In this passage, Grade walks the seven streets of the former Jewish quarter.

Return …

Since my return to Vilna, I have roamed
through the seven little alleys that once
made up the Ghetto. The narrow alleyways
enmesh and imprison me, like subterranean
passages, like caves filled with ancient
graves. Orphaned, they cast a spell upon
me; their emptiness hovers in my brain,
they attach themselves to me like seven
chains of stone. Yet I have no desire to
free myself of them. I want them to carve
themselves still deeper into my body, into
my flesh. I feel the dark, icy stiffness of
bolted gates and doors creep under my
skin. Shattered windows stare out through
my eyes, and someone inside me cries
aloud:

   "So be it! I want to become a ruin! …"

This inner cry comes from the *dybbuk* — the spirit of the ruins. Since my return, he has taken up residence within me, and I am no longer master of my thoughts, or even of my lips. The demon within speaks on and on, without end. I hear every word he utters, I implore him to be still; but his lamentations continue, at times as a wild outcry, at times with bitter calm, as of a mourner grown hoarse from wailing. And then, just when I want him to shout and lament, he falls silent, and his silence is so loud it deafens me — a terrifying silence, the furtive silence of a criminal, of an arsonist, as if it were he who had set all the fires in the Ghetto.

Now he speaks, the *dybbuk* within: Woe unto me that I have returned here. There, in Central Asia, there are snow-capped mountains; here, razed houses. I walk across paving stones, and it feels as if I am walking across a pavement of heads. Every stone has a different face, a different mask. How much better to have the sands of Kara Kum blowing in my face, or to look upon the saksaul tree of the desert, with its twisted branches and crippled trunk, than to hold in the palms of my hands the ashes of the Ghetto, or to gaze at a tall black chimney which, like me, stares up at the sky and, like me, asks: Why? If only just once a wind howled in the chimney! But even the wind lies poisoned, slaughtered all is empty, still, dead. When I was a child I heard my mother say that in a ruin, evil spirits dance. Would that I might come upon a band of demons ... at least then I would see that there is a Hell, then I would know that there is a reckoning.

All that is left is walls, roofs, pillars, cornices, tottering beams. All that is left is broken iron bedsteads, the rusty entrails of Primus stoves, twisted forks, knives, spoons-without the mouths. And I am left with eyes without tears, like window-holes with neither frames nor glass. I cannot squeeze even a single tear from my eyes, just as not even a single solitary Jew sticks his head out a window-hole. Behold! An entire row of shops, shuttered and bolted; an entire street with locked gates and doors. I think I hear laughter-behind one of the bolted gates someone is stifling his laughter, or perhaps choking on a consumptive cough.

"Open up, you brigand, open up!"

No one laughs, no one coughs, no one answers.

Thus does the demon within me rage without respite, cry out unceasingly, beat with my fists against the locked gates; and the slaughtered alleys answer with a moan, aggrieved at this disturbance of their deathly rest. For days on end, and half the nights, I drag myself through the same seven alleys of the Second Ghetto

– the 'Great' Ghetto. There had been a 'Small' Ghetto, too – the First Ghetto, consisting of the Synagogue Courtyard and a few surrounding alleys. The Germans had slaughtered the Jews who lived there four years ago, and the entire area has remained desolate ever since. Even my *dybbuk* is afraid to drag me over there. That was where my mother lived.

More than once it has happened that, sunk deep in thought, I have come upon the Ghetto's exit way, where the gate had been; one step more – and I shall be on the other side. It is dusk. Here among the ruins it grows dark earlier than anywhere else. From here the darkness spreads into the city, where people are strolling, talking and laughing. Vilna is gradually coming back to life. In the distance I hear the heavy, measured steps of soldiers. A military band begins to play and the soldiers sing. Those marchers and singers are the victors, but the Ghetto has not lived to see the victory. Hastily I turn back into the narrow streets. I am the guardian who may not leave. I hear the eerie silence asking me: "Watchman, what of the night? Watchman, what of the night?" And the spirit of the ruins who dwells within me answers: "Here the day is as dead and desolate as the night. Here the week is made up of seven Sabbaths, seven Sabbaths for seven alleys. But the Sabbath here is the Sabbath of Retribution – a Sabbath accursed eternally."

"And what do you seek here? What more are you waiting for?" asks the mysterious stillness, and the accursed one inside me begins once more to wail softly: "I am waiting for the moon to rise and to spin, from its cold rays, the silvery beard of an old Jew who will lean his head out a window toward me. Or perhaps, fluttering down a broken staircase will come a young

251

Jewish girl in a white nightgown woven
of moonlight. With her long black hair
unbound she will run out from her hiding
place, embrace me and cling to me. Or
perhaps someone is still alive in a hide-out
and cannot believe that the day of salvation
has come. Let him, this man driven mad
with fear, emerge now from his living
grave to laugh with a hollow, subterranean
laughter. He will laugh – and I will
shudder. I want to shudder! I want to be
shaken!"

But the moon avoids the Ghetto, and
the nocturnal spectres spun from my sickly
fantasies do not reveal themselves to me.

The narrow alleys grow pitch-dark.
From a street-lamp at the Ghetto's exit
falls a red ray of light, pointing toward me
like a bloody knife. Something rustles at
my feet: a bunch of crumpled stray leaves
from prayer books and Bibles, scattered
pages from volumes of commentaries. The

Ghetto has long since been exterminated,
but these pages of sacred books are still
strewn about, as though the dead return
at night to immerse themselves in their
tomes. After reading each page, the dead
scholars tear it out and give it over to the
wind, to bring to me so that I may see
what has become of the People of the Book.
I pick up the torn leaves and stuff my
pockets with them. When I return to my
lodging, I shall sort them out and smooth
out each one. Perhaps I shall recognize the
fingers that crumpled them. Perhaps I shall
hear the voice of the scholar who involved
himself in the Talmudic disputation
between the sages Abbaye and Rabbah.
Perhaps the tears that have been absorbed
by the pages of the women's prayer books
will glisten again for me. Perhaps my own
childish face will glow anew for me, and
I will be able once more to dream over a
book of miracle tales.

... By now the *dybbuk* within me
is weary unto death; I try to rouse him,
but he seems too dazed and exhausted
to answer. At last I can go home. I live
on Giedyminowska Street, in a Gentile
neighbourhood that has remained
untouched, the residence also of the other
Jews who have returned to Vilna. I drag
myself along the dark streets, followed by
houses with windows that have no panes,
by empty walls and smoke blackened
chimneys, by crooked roofs and maimed
dwelling-places a throng of cripples, a host
of blind beggars who feel their way with
their hands.

Across the cobbles toned pavement
of one dark Ghetto street a shaft of light
falls and bars my way. I spring aside as if
I have stepped on the body of a living Jew
who has just crawled out from some secret
hiding place. The light is seeping out
from a cellar window, close to the ground.

In the window hangs a black boot with a
pointed tip-the sign of a shoemaker. I peer
in: he appears to be a Jew. The slow, sleepy
hammering in the cellar drifts toward me
with a familiar warmth, and impels me
to descend to see who this workman is. I
feel for the door and walk down several
slippery, half-broken steps. My nostrils are
assailed by a smell of mildew, decay, and
filth. I open the lower door that leads into
the cellar, and the smoky kerosene lamp,
suspended by a wire above the cobbler's
workbench, becomes agitated. Its flame
blazes up, begins to jump and quiver, as
though it is happy to see me, the midnight
guest.[23]

The pain and tragedy seeps from every sentence. Yet
perhaps Grade's is simply a well written and more
poetically constructed version of what thousands of
returning Jews attempted to say on their journeys of
return.

Rivers

Maps of Jewish geography look their best when following the routes of rivers, especially in the light of the ever changing borders in the world. Rivers have defined the routes of Jewish settlement, trade and economy. Such was the connection of Jews to the river Vistula in Poland that the writer Sholem Asch wrote that it 'whispered in Yiddish' and behaved in a Jewish way. Yet rivers are also a natural part of nature. Despite its largely legalistic nature, the Talmud offers a beautiful tale of that interaction.

> Once R. Pinchas ben Yair was on his way to redeem captives, and came to the river Ganai. "O Ganai", said he, "divide your waters for me that I may pass through." It replied, "You are about to do the will of your Maker; I too am doing the will of my Maker. You may or may not accomplish your purpose, but I am sure of accomplishing mine." He said, "If you do not divide yourself, I will decree that no

256

waters ever pass through you." It thereupon
divided itself for him. There was also
present a certain man who was carrying
wheat for Passover, and so R. Pinchas once
again addressed the river. "Divide yourself
for this man as well, for he is engaged in a
religious duty." It thereupon divided itself
for him too. There was also an Arab who
had joined them [on the journey] and so
R. Pinchas once again addressed the river.
"Divide yourself for this man as well that
he may not say, "Is this the treatment of a
fellow traveler?" It thereupon divided itself
for him too [24]

Rabbi Pinchas ben Yair is on a journey to fulfill the
commandment of paying ransom to secure release of
captives or slaves, and is apparently joined by others
who all need to cross the same river. The ensuing conversation between rabbi and river revolves around the
purpose of their creation: the river to flow continually
and unthinkingly from one place to another; whilst

for the rabbi it is to play a direct and active role in the betterment of society and other people's lives. He goes further by joining his needs to those of his fellow travellers, ensuring that society can live and flourish. The man needing to bake *matzot* (unleavened bread) for Passover must be helped, as must the Arab to ensure good relations between the two communities.

It is a wonderful tale, locating at its centre an argument between Man and Nature, the 'journeyer' (Rabbi Pinchas) and the path of the journey (the river). It is rare in travel literature to find the 'journey' itself giving voice to an idea, but here it allows the traveler the chance to set the record straight. The world, according to Jewish tradition, should not be the predetermined course of direction, but the chosen path of what is right.

Ships and Trains

In the history of Jewish journeys, ships are the traditional mode of transport: captives leaving Israel for Rome; exiles departing from Spain and in more modern times, emigrants heading to the New World.

Returning to the image of the emigrants and families on the docks in Odessa as described in the previous chapter, the ship is a symbol of the transition between worlds. As vehicles for leaving and arriving, ships allow Jews more time for contemplation and change. A Jewish journey literature of the aeroplane would just be too quick in order for it to work as well.

Jacob Glatstein's 1938 novel *Ven Yash iz Geforn* ('When Yash Went Forth') reverses the direction of the conventional Jewish journey of the time, travelling from America back to Europe. Having left Poland in 1914 aged eighteen, Glatstein had himself returned to his native Lublin twenty years later, only to be shocked at the rise of anti Semitism that he saw there. The novel reflects more than the political tides of the European continent and tells of the inner journey of the writer, caught up as he was between the two worlds.

Most of the novel takes place aboard ship, a space within which Yash (Glatstein), is able to confront the meaning of the journey, recalling as he does for a significant section of the book, his previous journey in the other direction. Yet with time and new experience, the author is really looking for a re-evaluation of both places. Unlike his enthusiastic youthful departure earlier he is now drawn back to the place of roots.

> As the liner eased from the pier, I looked
> for a remote secluded nook in which to
> struggle with the conflicting emotions
> deep within me.
>
> Like exotic sea plants the red, yellow
> and green lights of small craft flirted with
> our vessel, which was creating an ever
> increasing sphere of loneliness about itself.
>
> To flee more quickly the sentimental
> reminders of relatives, family and terra
> firma!
>
> The *Olympic* promptly broke loose from
> the earth and became a small planet with
> its own inhabitants, civilisation, and even
> invisible director, whose existence might
> be denied if one so desired.

The ship provides the place for the returning Glatstein to meet, observe and talk with people from all walks of life and locations. There are Jews and non-Jews, all of whom allow him the opportunity to reflect on his own view of the world. As the book draws to a close, he boards a train on the final section of the journey where he meets a special character, a Pole, who will sharpen the focus of his self-reflection.

> A young man of some twenty-odd years
> entered my compartment. He bowed and
> sat down opposite me at the window,
> which kept focusing bits of forest, field,
> stream and summer sky of dull blue. An
> indifferent sky – it was clear at once that
> there would be neither lightning, thunder,
> nor rain all that wearisome day.
>
> The slender young man smiled amiably
> even before making up his mind to chat.
>
> I asked him to pardon my rusty Polish,
> explaining that it was the first time in
> twenty years that I had needed to recall it.

"Where from? A stranger?"

"No, but an expatriate. From New York".

"In that case you must put the receivers to your ears and be greeted by our music first of all."

He pointed to the radio earphones and I obediently put them on.

The train sped onward, and with it the squeak of trashy café tunes which greeted my ears. However, I was thankful to him for his suggestion. The common Polish songs and their insane words had an inherent charm, were no less different than the Polish panorama – the grass, groves and valleys which were fleeting by.

"Magnificent", I exclaimed, "the total flora and fauna of the land."

"That indeed," said he beaming, "Our poverty, our joy, and our sorrow. Our own."

He began to polish his spectacles and peered at me with lacklustre light brown

eyes. Without the glasses they appeared
sullen, but were made radiant by a smile.
Twenty years ago I had seen few such faces
among the youth of Poland. It was a far
cry from the flaxen haired peasant lad
with foolish eyes and pimply face to this
European visage opposite me. This refined
face had been raised in the atmosphere of a
fatherland.

I conveyed all this to him in careful
phrases, even the comparison to the peasant
lad of the past. I assured him that I was as
thankful for his musical welcome as for his
aspect. It was new and different.

His brow furrowed and I sensed
his anxiety. This young man, I mused
had an almost Jewish hump on his
back; ours was born of Jewish exile,
his under the burden of a young land,
young government with all the ills and
afflictions of infancy. He was wearing the
yoke of responsible citizenship.

"We are working to raise Poland's prestige in the world."

He again removed his eye glasses and began wiping them, but this time in order to avoid my gaze. "You're a Jew, aren't you?" He said *zhid* but it was spoken softly, without any venom. "There are some among us who drag the fine traditions of Poland to the ground. That's an excrescence. We shall cut it out."

He offered me a firm hand as if solemnly taking a sacred vow. We understood each other and discussed it no further …

… "My mother's very ill," I explained and the thought suddenly flashed through my mind: Is she still alive?

The sun parched grass appeared to be sailing by the window. An old dog barked at the train. A small sombre lad waived his cap. A thick copse seized hold of the sun and splattered it into a thousand specks of lights, gilding the trees.

My companion suddenly glanced at his watch and his face lit up.

"Another half an hour and you reach your goal. Exactly thirty-two minutes – why, not even thirty-two minutes!"

He grew increasingly excited at the prospect.

"Of twenty years of self exile, there remain" – his watch was in his hand – "precisely thirty-one minutes."

… "Man, you have about two or three minutes more! Perhaps not even that!"

There were several long blasts of the locomotive whistle. At first, factory chimneys appeared and then a number of huts surrounded by gardens. It was already near nightfall and the ramshackle but neat houses were mirroring themselves in the cooler rays of the sun.

The Polish youth was standing at my side, his hand on my shoulder as if to make easier for me the last weary minute.

There were tears in his eyes. The train was
coming to a stop. Simultaneously with
the conductor the young Pole sang out
joyously:

   "*Lublin*!"[25]

As 'Yash Went Forth' as the title declares, what does
his journey represent? It is a homecoming complete
with recognition of familiar landscape. More significantly, he encounters the complex question of the
new Poland with its enthusiastic supporter who joins
and even becomes part of the homecoming. Central
to his sharing the excitement is the presentation of
time – twenty years of exile versus 32 minutes on
the train. Finally, Glatstein poses the ambiguous
question of the meaning of arrival. Having left on
the ship to withdraw into himself, the book closes
with his arrival. Will it bring the understanding and
completion he seeks or not?

Trains seem to define the modern world, their
powerful engines symbolize change. Throughout the
nineteenth century the old and slow road was under-

mined as railway tracks redirected the route of travel. Whole towns and economies were weakened as the trade and industry refocused its sights. It is therefore fitting that the Yiddish writer Sholem Aleichem (1859–1916) should have turned his attention to this subject despite being better known for his stories of Tevye the Dairyman, popularized by Hollywood in the film 'Fiddler on the Roof'. Outwardly, his writings are of the rooted communities of East European Jews, mostly in small *shtetlech* and towns where their characters and cultures flourish. Yet, the real drama lies in the confrontations between the Jews and their changing environment.

'The Railway Stories' (*Di ayznban-geshikhtes*) is a collection of tales and sketches narrated by a salesman travelling in the third class compartment of a train. The setting alone is poignant given the turbulent nature of the time; set when Russia is slowly confronting the modern world. The constant movement, the comings and goings of the train provides the backdrop to the stories, further reinforcing the idea of the train as the very symbol of change. Unlike the settled location of his other stories, such as the *shtetl* of Kasrilevke, here the Jews are moving, caught up in the modern world, its technologies, its encroachment on traditional space and the undermining of old locations that were once sustained by the traffic of horse-drawn transport. In fact all aspects of relations are changed in the setting of the third class compartment. At first they appear to be cosy and warm, as opposed to the silent and disengaged world of first class. Yet, as geography is conquered by the train's movement, it becomes clear that all is not entirely as it seems.

Third Class (1902)
This is not so much a story as a little chat,
a few words of admonition and farewell
from a good friend. As we are about to
part, dear reader, I would like to show
my gratitude for your having borne with
me for so long by giving you some useful
advice, the fond counsel of a practical man.
Listen carefully.

If you must go somewhere by train, especially if the trip is a long one, and you wish to have the feeling of travelling, that is, of having enjoyed the experience, avoid going first or second class.

First class, of course, is out of the question anyway. God protect you from it! Naturally, I'm not referring to the ride itself. The ride in first class is far from unpleasant – indeed, it's sumptuous, comfortable, roomy, and with every possible convenience. It's not that I'm talking about; it's the people, the passengers. What can be the point, I ask you, of a Jew travelling in total solitude without a living soul to speak to? By the time you've reached your destination, you can have forgotten how to use your voice! And even if once in a blue moon you happen to run into another passenger, it's either some vulgar country squire with crimson jowls like a trombonist's, or some

269

stuck-up lady who's as sniffy as a mother-
in-law, or some foreign tourist in checked
pants whose eyes are glued so tightly to
the window that not even a fire in the car
could tear him away from it. When you
travel with such types, you begin to have
the most depressing thoughts – why, you
may even find yourself ruminating about
death. Who needs it?

Do you think second class is any better,
though? There you are, surrounded by
all sorts of people who are obviously no
different from yourself, with the identical
human passions. They would like nothing
better than to talk to you; in fact, they're
dying of curiosity to know where you're
going, where you're from, and who you
are; but they sit there like so many tailor's
dummies and so do you, and all that
happens is one big exchange of stares.
The whole car has taken a vow of silence
– shhh, watch out you don't break it!

For example: across from you is a young dandy with manicured nails and a smart moustache whom you could swear you know from someplace, you just can't remember where. Indeed, he shows every sign of stemming from Mosaic lineage, that is, of being a fellow tribesman of yours. What good does that do you, though, when you can't get a word out of him? He's finished twirling the ends of his moustache, and now all he wants is to look out the window and whistle.

If you'd like to take a few good years off such a person's life – in fact, bury him so thoroughly that not even the Resurrection can put him back on his feet – all you need to do, provided there's a Christian sitting next to him, or better yet, a young lady, is turn to him in any language at all, though Russian is preferable, and inquire, *"Yesli ya nye oshibayus, ya imyel udovolstvye vstryetitsa s'vami v'Berdichevye?"* (In Yiddish

271

we would say, "If I'm not mistaken, didn't I once have the pleasure of meeting you in Berdichev?") Believe me, that's a thousand times worse than any name you might call his father!

On the other hand, if you run into such a type in Podolia or Volhynia, Polish might be the better gambit. *"Pszepraszam, Pana! "Jesli sie nie myle znalem ojca Pana z Jarmelyncu, ktory byl w laskach u jasnie wielmoizego Potokego?"* (Roughly speaking that's, "Excuse me, sir, but if my memory doesn't betray me, I'm an old friend of your father's from Yarmelinetz; wasn't he in the service of Count Potocki there?") That may not seem like any great insult, but Yarmelinetz and the service of Count Potocki just happen to spell J-e-w …

When you travel third class, on the other hand, you feel right at home. In fact, if you happen to be in a car whose passengers are exclusively Jews, you may

feel a bit too much at home. Granted,
third class is not the height of luxury; if
you don't use your elbows, you'll never
find a seat, the noise level, the sheer
hubbub, is ear-splitting; you can never
be sure where you end and where your
neighbours begin ... and yet there's no
denying that that's an excellent way to
meet them. Everyone knows who you are,
where you're bound for, and what you do,
and you know the same about everyone.
At night you can save yourself the bother
of having to fall asleep, because there's
always someone to talk to – and if you're
not in the mood to talk, someone else will
be glad to do it for you. Who expects to
sleep on a train ride anyway? Talking is
far better, because you never know what
may come of it. I should only live another
year of my life for each time I've seen
perfect strangers on the train end up by
making a business deal, arranging a match

273

for their children, or learning something worth knowing from each other.

For instance, all the talk you hear about doctors, indigestion, sanatoriums, toothaches, nervous conditions, Karlsbad, and so forth – you'd think it was all just a lot of malarkey, wouldn't you? Well, let me tell you a story about that. Once I was travelling with a group of Jews. We were talking about doctors and prescriptions. At the time, it shouldn't happen to you, I was having problems with my stomach, and a fellow passenger, a Jew from Kamenetz, recommended a medicine that came in the form of a powder. It so happened, said the Jew, that he had been given this powder by a dentist rather than a doctor, but the powder, which was yellow, was absolutely first-rate. That is, it wasn't yellow, it was white, like all powders; but it came in a yellow wrapper. He even swore to me by everything that was holy,

the Jew did, that he owed his life to the
yellow powder, because without it – no,
he didn't even want to think of it! And
I didn't need to use a whole lot, either.
Two or three grains, he said, would make
me feel like a new man; no more stomach
aches, and no more money-grubbing, blood
sucking physicians; I could say to hell with
everyone of the damn quacks! "If you'd
like," he said, "I can give you two or three
grains of my yellow powder right now.
You'll never stop thanking me ..."

And that's what he did. I came home, I
took one, two, three grains of the stuff, and
after a while – it didn't happen at once, but
later on, in the middle of the night – I had
such pains that I thought I was kicking the
bucket. I swear, I was sure I was on my last
gasp! A doctor was called, and then another
– it was all they could do to bring me back
from death's door ... Well, now I know that
if a Jew from Kamenetz tries giving you a

yellow powder, you should tell him to take
a powder himself. Every lesson has its price.

When you go third class and wake up
in the morning to discover that you've
left your *tefillin* and your prayer shawl
at home, there isn't any cause for alarm
– you only need to ask and you'll be given
someone else's, along with whatever else
you require. All that's expected of you in
return, once you're done praying, is to
open your suitcase and display your own
wares. Vodka, cake, a hard-boiled egg, a
drumstick, a piece of fish – it's all grist
for the mill. Perhaps you have an apple,
an orange, a piece of strudel? Out with it,
no need to be ashamed! Everyone will be
glad to share it with you, no one stands
on ceremony here. A train ride and good
company, you understand, are two things
that create an appetite … And of course, if
you happen to have a wee bit of wine with
you, there's no lack of volunteer tasters,

each with his own verdict and name for it. "It's a Bessarabian muscat," says one. "No, it's an imported Akerman," says another. "What kind of muscat?" says a third, getting angrily to his feet. "What kind of Akerman? Can't you tell it's a Koveshaner Bordeaux?" At which point a fourth fellow rises from his corner with the smile of a true connoisseur, accepts the glass of wine with an expression that says, "Stand back, you duffers, this calls for an expert," takes a few sips, and pronounces, his cheeks flushed a merrymaker's red:

"Jews, do you know what this is? No, I can see that you don't It's neither more nor less than a pure, simple, honest, no-nonsense, homemade Berdichev kiddush wine!"

And everyone realizes that the man is right, a Berdichev kiddush wine it is. And since quite a few tongues have been loosened by the time the wine has made its rounds, suddenly everyone is telling everybody everything, and everything is being told to everyone. The whole car is talking together at once in a splendid show of Jewish solidarity. Before long each of us not only knows all about the others' troubles, he knows about every trial and tribulation that ever befell a Jew anywhere. It's enough to warm the cockles of your heart!

When you travel third class and arrive in some town and don't know where to stay, you have a car full of Jews to help you out. In fact, the number of different places recommended will tally exactly with the number of Jews in the car. "The Hotel Frankfurt," says one of them, singing the praises of his choice. "It's bright and it's cheery, it's clean and it's breezy, it's the biggest bargain in town." "The Hotel Frankfurt?" exclaims someone else. "God forbid! It's dark and it's dreary,

it's sordid and sleazy, it's the biggest gyp
joint around. If you really want to enjoy
yourself, I suggest you try the Hotel New
York," "The only reason I can think of
for staying in the New York," puts in
another traveller, "is that you're homesick
for bedbugs. Here, hand me your bag and
come with me to my favourite, the Hotel
Russia. It's the only place for a Jew!"

Of course, having given him your bag
you had better keep an eye on him to make
sure he doesn't make off with it ... but I
ask you, where in this wonderful world of
ours aren't there thieves nowadays? Either
you're fated to meet up with one or you're
not. If it's in your crystal ball to be robbed,
you can be cleaned out in broad daylight,
and no amount of prayers or policemen will
make the slightest difference. If anything,
you'll thank your lucky stars that you got
away with your life ...

In a word, go third class. Those are the

parting words to you of a good friend and a
practical man, a commercial traveller.

Adieu![26]

The train is a new departure for Sholem Aleichem,
replacing the intimate and rooted world of the *shtetl*.
Despite the surface warmth of the narrator it is clear
that no new community has come to replace it. As the
train keeps moving, there are echoes of the previous
small-world culture but the people are becoming
more disconnected from each other. The railroad is
a place where people observe and tell others of their
lives knowing that the listeners will soon get off.
This is a pragmatic and transient community, which
unlike the characters of Sholem Aleichem's other
works, appear to have no roots.

Airports

For the contemporary traveller, airports cut to the
heart of the drama. Everyone is moving, meeting
periodically in transient spaces before heading off
in a definite direction. And so they are good places

to engage in dialogue since one is vulnerable and in motion. The passage below, by the writer Sami Shalom Chetrit, speaks to the essence of the dialogue, albeit a confused one. Chetrit was born in Qasr as-Suq in Morocco, emigrated to Israel and has spent long periods in the United States.

Getting to know a friendly American Jew: Conversation

Tell me, you're from Israel?

Yes, I'm from there.

Oh, and where in Israel do you live?

Jerusalem. For the last few ears I have lived there.

Oh, Jerusalem is such a beautiful city.

And do you … you're from West … or East …

That's a tough question, depends on whose drawing the map.

You're funny, and do you, I mean do you speak Hebrew?

Yes, of course.

I mean, that's your mother tongue?

Not really. My mother's tongue is Arabic; but
  now she speaks Hebrew fine.
Oh 'ze yofi', I learned that in the Kibbutz.
Not bad at all.
And you are, I mean, you're Israeli right?
Yes of course.
Your family observant?
Pretty much.
Do they keep the Sabbath?
Me, no depends, actually …
Do you eat pork?
No, that no.
Excuse me for prying, but I just have to ask you,
  are you Jewish or Arab?
I'm an Arab Jew.
You're funny.
No, I'm quite serious.
Arab Jew? I've never heard of that.
It's simple: Just the way you say you're an
  American Jew. Here, try to say
"European Jews."
"European Jews."

Now say "Arab Jews."

You can't compare, European Jews is something
    else.

How come?

Because "Jew" just doesn't go with "Arab", it
    just doesn't go. It doesn't even sound right.

Depends on your ear.

Look I've got nothing against Arabs. I even have
    friends who are Arabs, but how can you say
    "Arab Jew" when all the Arabs want is to
    destroy the Jews?

And how can you say "European Jew" when the
    Europeans have already destroyed the Jews?[27]

Israel

Journeys are about home.

As an immigrant, it is hard but not difficult to
see the challenge of defining home in the Israeli
literature of journeys. I did not flee persecution, did
not arrive as a penniless refugee but chose this as
my home and in so doing also accept the struggle
to reach the heart of Israeli society. It defines a

quintessentially Jewish and Israeli journey, between the periphery and the centre.

Yehuda Amichai, the much-loved poet of the Land of Israel and Jerusalem, is neither the idealistic celebrator of national 'return' nor the sombre poet of alienation. As the poet of the Land of Israel *par excellence*, his greatness lies in his ironic and earthy assumptions, constantly involved in creating dialogues between the people and the land. For him, all parts of the Jewish drama are holy; land, people; books and history, each in their own way. The journey lies in the encounter between them.

Sandals

Sandals are the skeleton of a whole shoe,
The skeleton, and its only true spirit.

Sandals are the reins of my galloping feet
And the tefillin straps
Of a tired foot, praying.

Sandals are the patch of private land I walk on

Everywhere I go, ambassadors of my homeland,
My true country, the skies
To small swarming creatures of the earth
And their day of destruction that's sure to come.

Sandals are the youth of the shoe
And a memory of walking in the wilderness.

I don't know when they'll lose me
Or when I'll lose them, but they will
Be lost, each in a different place:
One not far from my house
Among rocks and shrubs, the other
Sinking into the dunes near the Great Sea
Like a setting sun,
Facing a setting sun.[28]

'Sandals' reflects a desire to go beyond the formal symbols of the Israeli journey; that of Biblical landscapes, immigrants and wars. Instead, the symbol is more prosaic, a pair of sandals. If the wanderer's staff or the bundle of clothes represents the medieval

Jewish traveller, the pair of sandals is the icon of the Israeli. Down to earth and straightforward, they symbolise the *tiyul* (hike), the desert and the relationship between new Jew and their land.

Amichai's advantage in choosing his symbols lies in his status as insider. Born in Germany, he emigrated at the age of eleven and became a fighter in the élite Palmach at the age of 22. His journey to the land of Israel fitted an official narrative and favouritism enjoyed by European-born élites in comparison to other Europeans. Therefore it should not be surprising to find a parallel of journey literature by those obliged to travel a greater distance to penetrate the inner reaches of Israeli society.

As an Algerian-born *Mizrachi* (Oriental) Jew, Erez Biton's journey was more complicated, starting out as the cultural 'other'. Much of his work gives voice to those whose journey has resulted in one form of dislocation or another: cultural; emotional; economic; and political. Biton does not subvert the entire notion of Zionism, with its idealised journey of the 'Ingathering of the Exiles', but he does critique its reality. The poem 'Zohra al Fasiya' speaks through the experience of the legendary Jewish Moroccan singer of that name. Her journey to Israel has come at the expense of the fame and status she enjoyed in Morocco and is now a sad shadow of herself, bereft of her glory and living through her memories.

> ### Zohra al-Fasiya's Song
> *singer at Muhammad the Fifth's court in*
>   *Rabat, Morocco*
> *they say when she sang*
> *soldiers fought with knives*
> *to clear a path through the crowd*
> *to reach the hem of her skirt*
> *to kiss the tips of her toes*
> *to leave her a piece of silver as a sign of thanks*
>
> *Zohra al-Fasiya*
>
> *now you can find her in Ashkelon*
> *Antiquities 3*
> *by the welfare office the smell*

of leftover sardine cans on a wobbly three-legged
   table
the stunning royal carpets stained on the Jewish
   Agency cot
spending hours in a bathrobe
in front of the mirror
with cheap make-up

when she says

   Muhammad Cinque

   apple of our eyes

you don't really get it at first

Zohra al-Fasiya's voice is hoarse
her heart is clear
her eyes are full of love

Zohra al-Fasiya [29]

Home

Finally, as if to illustrate the complicated implications of journeys, the Talmud offers the following story.

> ... Rav Rahumei frequently [studied]
> before Rava [his teacher] in Mahoza. He
> regularly came home every Yom Kippur
> eve: One day his studies captivated him.
> His wife was looking out for him, saying
> "Now he is coming, Now he is coming".
> He did not come. She became distressed
> and a tear fell from her eye. He was sitting
> on a roof. The roof collapsed under him
> and he died.[30]

This intriguing tale revolves around two journeys, the first of Rav Rahumei who has chosen to study away from home in a Babylonian academy and the second of his annual journey home to see his wife. Why would Rav Rahumei choose studies over his wife in the first place? How does the distance between them (and the assumptions underlying such decisions) affect their love? It would seem that his wife could sustain the love, illustrated by her excited waiting (i.e. 'Now he is coming, Now he is coming'). She does not know that he has allowed distance to reveal a greater love for his studies than her. His journey has taken him closer to learning but further away from his wife, for which the text condemns him.

Epilogue

The story is told of Ayzik of Krakow, the son of Reb Yekl who dreamt night after night of a great treasure that lay hidden under the Praga Bridge that crossed the Vistula in Warsaw. Unable to ignore his dream any longer, Reb Ayzik journeyed to the city believing his prayers would be answered. As he searched unsuccessfully, a soldier stopped him, demanding an explanation for Reb Ayzik's strange behaviour. Upon hearing of this fruitless journey in search of treasure he laughed, and replied, 'If I dreamt of a great treasure in the oven in the house of Reb Ayzik of Krakow, do you think I would have to drop everything to seek it out.' Thereupon, Reb Ayzik turned around to begin the journey home. There in his oven in Krakow lay a great treasure.

Not all journeys yield great riches. Paradoxically, journeys are sometimes required to appreciate this.

Endnotes

Self: Personal Reflections on Jewish Journeys

1. From 'Jewish Travel' in Yehuda Amichai, *Open, Closed Open*, translated by Chana Bloch and Chana Kronfeld (Harcourt Inc, Florida: 2000) p 117.

2. Bernard Malamud, *The Fixer* (Eyre & Spottiswoode, London: 1967) p 17.

Context: The Idea of Journey in Jewish Experience

1. Exodus 12: 42.

2. Exodus 13: 3–8.

3. Exodus 13: 17–22.

4. R. Meir Simchah Ha-Cohen of Dvinsk, *Meshech Hochmah*, commenting on Exodus 30: 11–34:35 (1927).

5. From 'Jewish Travel' in Yehuda Amichai, *Open, Closed Open*, translated by Chana Bloch and Chana Kronfeld (Harcourt Inc, Florida: 2000) p 117.

6. Babylonian Talmud, Berachot 29b.

7. Deuteronomy 26: 4–9.

8. Psalm 137.

9. Jeremiah 29: 1–7, 10.

10. Psalm 126.

11. Elkan Nathan Adler (ed), *Jewish Travellers in the Middle Ages* (Dover Publications, New York: 1987) p 189 [originally *Jewish Travellers* (George Routledge & Sons Ltd, London: 1930].

12. Shulchan Aruch, Orah Haim 560.

13. Gershon Bader, *Drasig Dores Yidn in Poilen* (1927) quoted in Haya Bar-Itzhak, *Jewish Poland: Legends of Origin* (Wayne State University Press, Detroit: 2001) p 147.

14. Steve Israel, *Exile 1492: the Expulsion of the Jews from Spain* (Ben-Zvi Institute, Jerusalem: 1992) p 147.

15. Translated by Dr Barbara Garvin in Howard Schwartz & Anthony Rudolph (ed), *Voices within the*

Ark (Avon Books, New York: 1980) p 1043.

16. Count Miklos Zay, *Jews in Society* (*Zsidok a tarsadolomban*) (Haszadik Szazad, Budapest: 1904), quoted in Geza Komoroczy (ed), *Jewish Hungary* (Eötvös Lóránd University, Andrea Strbik, CEU Press, Budapest: 1999).

17. Franz Kafka to Milena Jesenska (1920), quoted in Harald Salfellner, *Franz Kafka and Prague* (Vitalis, Prague: 2003) pp 169–71.

18. Reprinted from Richard J. Fein (ed), *Selected Poems of Yankev Glatshteyn* (The Jewish Publication Society: 1987).

19. Isaiah 11:12.

20. Hana Wirth-Nesher, 'After the Sound and Fury: An Interview', *Prooftexts 2* (1982) p 312.

21. From 'Railroad Agents' by Assaf Tzipor and the Cameri Quintet, printed in *Ha'aretz* 30 April 2004.

Voices and Places: Literary Jewish Journeys through the Ages

1. Ludwig Zamenhof, in a letter to N Borovko (1895) quoted in Majorie Boulton, *Zamenhof: Creator*

of Esperanto (Routledge and Kegan Paul, London: 1960) p 6.

2. Genesis 28: 10–13

3. Rashi, commentary on Genesis 28:12.

4. Jonah 1–3:2.

5. Babylonian Talmud, Shabbat 56b.

6. E. Natali, *Il Ghetto di Roma* (Rome: 1887) p 1.

7. Jerusalem Talmud, Avodah Zara 40a.

8. Czeslaw Milosz, from Milton Teichman and Sharon Leder (eds), *Truth and Lamentation* (University of Illinois Press: 1994) p 303.

9. Elkan Nathan Adler (ed), *Jewish Travellers in the Middle Ages* (Dover Publications, New York: 1987) pp 38, 43–4 [originally *Jewish Travellers* (George Routledge & Sons Ltd, London: 1930)].

10. Rabbi Moses ben Nahman, reprinted from Reuven Hammer, *The Jerusalem Anthology: A Literary Guide* (The Jewish Publication Society: 1995).

11. Yehuda Halevi, 'The Poet is Urged to Remain in Spain', in *The Jewish Poets of Spain*, translated by David Goldstein (Penguin, London: 1971) p 137.

12. Yehuda Halevi, translated by Raymond S.

Scheindlin, from David Biale (ed), *Cultures of the Jews* (Schocken, New York: 2002) pp 375–6.

13. Yehuda Amichai, 'Ecology of Jerusalem,' in *Selected Poems* (Penguin, London: 1988, originally UK Viking: 1987) p 136.

14. Leo W. Schwarz, *Memoirs of my People* (Rinehart & Company, New York: 1943) pp 46–7.

15. Alexandra Richie, *Faust's Metropolis: A History of Berlin* (HarperCollins, London: 1999) p xvii.

16. Solomon Maimon, *Solomon Maimon: An Autobiography* (Schocken, New York: 1947) pp 56–62. Translation J. Clark Murray, 1888.

17. From 'Ghettoes in the West' in Joseph Roth, *The Wandering Jews* (English translation 2001 by W.W. Norton & Company Inc, New York. 2001) pp 80–2, 84–5.

18. Poems by Yankev Yitzchok Segal in Irving Howe, Ruth Wisse & Khone Shmeruk, *Penguin Book of Modern Yiddish Verse* (Viking, London: 1987) p 420.

19. Mordechai Gebirtig, original in YIVO Institute for Jewish Research, New York.

20. Survivor testimony, Yad Vashem archive.

21. Elie Wiesel, *Night* (Penguin, London: 1981) pp 39, 40.

22. Lucy S. Dawidowicz, *From that Time and Place: A memoir 1938–1947* (W.W. Norton & Company, New York: 1989) pp 121–2.

23. Excerpt from Chaim Grade, 'The Seven Little Alleys', in *My Mother's Sabbath Days* (Schocken, New York: 1987) pp 235–7, 238–9.

24. Babylonian Talmud, Hullin 7a.

25. Jacob Glatstein, *Homeward Bound* (originally "When Yash Went Forth'), translated by Abraham Goldstein (Thomas Yoseloff Publ., New York: 1969) p 137.

26. Excerpt from Sholem Aleichem, *Tevye the Dairyman and the Railroad Stories*, translated by Hillel Halkin (Library of Yiddish Classics, Schocken, New York: 1987) pp 279–84.

27. Sami Shalom Chetrit from Ammiel Alcalay (ed), *Keys to the Garden: New Israeli Writing* (City Lights Books, San Francisco: 1996) pp 362–3. Translation by Ammiel Alcalay.

28. Translated by Chana Bloch, in Yehuda Amichai, *Selected Poems* (Penguin, London: 1988, originally UK Viking: 1987) pp 155–6.

29. From Ammiel Alcalay (ed), *Keys to the Garden: New Israeli Writing* (City Lights Books, San Francisco: 1996) p 267. Translation Ammiel Alcalay.

30. Babylonian Talmud, Ketubot 62b.

Acknowledgements

This book would not have been possible without the inspiration from the many people who have accompanied me on trips across the Jewish world over so many years. Participants on programmes, both real and imagined, have been the best people to try out ideas, hear feedback from and offer reflections on their own Jewish journeys.

In addition to these people, I am indebted to the following publishers for permission to quote from their publications: every effort was made to seek copyright for the poem 'A Roman Roman,' by Crescenzo del Monte, translated by Dr Barbara Garvin in *Voices within the Ark*, edited by Howard Schwartz & Anthony Rudolph (Avon Books, New York: 1980); excerpt by Benjamin of Tudela from *Jewish Travellers*

303

translated by Channa Goldstein, copyright © 1986 by the Estate of Chaim Grade. Used by permission of Alfred A. Knopf, a division of Random House, Inc.; poem 'Sandals' translated by Chana Bloch in *Selected Poems* by Yehuda Amichai (Viking Penguin UK: 1987). Reprinted with kind permission from the estate of Yehuda Amichai; poem 'Zohra al-Fasiya's Song' by Erez Biton and poem 'Getting to know a friendly American Jew: Conversation' by Sami Chetrit in *Keys to the Garden: New Israeli Writing* by Ammiel Alcalay (editor). Translation copyright 1996 by Ammiel Alcalay. Reprinted by permission of City Lights Books.

In addition to this very large group, there are also various friends and colleagues who have provided ideas and suggestions for this book and the journeys that inspired it. I am indebted to David Goldberg and Michael Wegier of the UJIA, Adam Minsky of UIA Canada, as well as the RSGB Living Judaism Project for their support for Jewish travel in Europe. Many thanks to Rabbi Joel Levy, Rabbi Gideon Sylvester, Robert Bogen as well as to excellent travel companions Jona Cummings and Richard Goldstein. Deep gratitude to two brilliant colleagues: Steve Israel for numerous suggestions, ideas, friendship and good grammar and Julian Resnick, my indefatigable Jewish Journeys partner.

Special thanks to my patient editor and more importantly true friend, Anne Joseph, without whom this book would never have been realized.

Lastly, thanks beyond words for their long-suffering acceptance of my absences, to Nikki, Noa, Ella and Tal.

Index

308

311